The Promise of Technology in Schools

The Next 20 Years

Charles K. Stallard
with
Julie S. Cocker

The Scarecrow Press, Inc.
A Scarecrow Education Book
Lanham, Maryland, and London
2001

SCARECROW PRESS, INC.

Published in the United States of America
by Scarecrow Press, Inc.
4720 Boston Way
Lanham, Maryland 20706
www.scarecrowpress.com

4 Pleydell Gardens, Folkestone
Kent CT20 2DN, England

British Cataloguing in Publication Information Available

Library of Congress Cataloging-in-Publication Data

Stallard, Charles K., 1942–
    The promise of technology in schools: the next 20 years / Charles K.
Stallard with Julie S. Cocker.
        p. cm. —(A Scarecrow education book)
    ISBN 0-8108-4082-0 (pbk. : alk. paper)
    1. Educational technology. 2. Information technology. I. Cocker, Julie S.,
1970– II. Title. III. Series

LB1028.3 .S735 2001
370'.285—dc21

                                                            2001040064

∞™ The paper used in this publication meets the minimum requirements
of American National Standard for Information Sciences—Permanence of
Paper for Printed Library Materials, ANSI/NISO Z39.48-1992.
Manufactured in the United States of America.

Contents

Introduction

> The status quo cannot be the way forward, nor will the status quo, slightly amended, be the best way forward.
>
> —Charles Handy

Since the arrival of microcomputers in the late 1970s, pressures have been building to use them as a catalyst for the reform of public education. Even the very early Commodore Pet seemed to afford benefits that schools and teachers just could not afford to miss. Now, at the beginning of a new century, K–12 education stands almost alone among institutions; exhibiting a remarkable resistance to the forces of transformation that the microcomputer brings with it. The future may well look back on the last quarter of the twentieth century in amazement at the ability of education to persevere in its traditional form and processes while the rest of the world moved on. Will it also look on the first two decades of the twenty-first century in the same way?

The ability of public and private K–12 education to maintain its traditional culture and resist substantive change makes any predictions of its future something of a gamble. In 1985, who would have thought so little change would have come about from the many technological resources that began pouring into schools at that time? There is now some indication that substantial change may be in the making. K–12 education is a subsystem of society after all. As such it will come, as it always has, to reflect the needs and character of the society it serves. Here at the dawn of the twenty-first century, educators and others are beginning to look with earnest for clues about how education will and should change. At the same time, local, state, and federal governments have stepped up funding in an attempt to establish levels of technology resources for schools needed to make transformation possible. If access to technology was a problem in the past, it should not stand in the way now.

What are the factors driving change today? Is it the technology itself? How much faster, smaller, and cheaper can computers be made? What are the internal obstacles to change that schools will have to overcome? Will schools be able to overcome these obstacles? Assuming that the transformation of K–12 education does happen, will the resulting system or systems of schools provide more or less service to society than the current model afforded the twentieth century? Questions such as these hint at the complexity underlying both the educational process and the technological advancements that are reshaping society.

Market forces have driven the development of information technologies within the private sector. That is not likely to change in the foreseeable future. What is the education technology market like, and how does it influence developments within the field of information technology, or IT, itself? Determining the future of educational technology will require an understanding of how public education as a market for technology products and services differs from other markets in both the private and public sectors. We will examine this in depth in chapter 4. Private K–12 education differs slightly from the public model and represents a sizeable market, but it will be public K–12 education that ultimately drives reform. In terms of market, size counts.

Determining the future of educational technology may seem impossible at first, but there are places to look for clues. When it comes to the transformational power of IT, K–12 education is now in a position occupied by others in the recent past. IT resources are beginning to arrive in schools in numbers and in configurations sufficient to support and maintain real change. Adding networks to the technological mix has brought a configuration of resources into schools that affords alternatives to instructional delivery. Until similar events happened in business, managers usually considered desktop computers distractions rather than engines of productivity. Infusions of funding from federal sources along with initiatives at the state level have placed billions of dollars of resources into the hands of students, teachers, and school administrators. This funding stream has been inconsistent to date, but even in this area there is growing evidence that legislators have come to recognize the importance of IT capabilities for all students and are now searching for the best ways to provide predictable funding on a long-term basis. What is not clear is whether public education will or should use these new resources to follow the same paths of transformation that have recast business, government, and the military in such a remarkably short time. The harder question for public education may be whether the system as we now know it should continue. The capabilities of today's technologies are showing ways to create entirely new and different approaches to teaching and learning. Central to this issue is the purpose of education in America.

THE PURPOSE OF EDUCATION

Education in America serves different purposes for different people and groups, but it is the role that it plays in the continuance of our society itself that ultimately sets goals and missions. In an 1818 report for the University of Virginia, Thomas Jefferson made the mission and goals for nineteenth-century American education clear. It is at once functional and imbued with the vision that gave rise to our culture and government:

> To give every citizen the information he needs for the transaction of his own business; to enable him to calculate for himself, and to express and preserve his ideas, his contracts and accounts in writing; to improve, by reading, his morals and faculties; to understand his duties to his neighbors and country, and to discharge with competence the functions confided to him by either; to know his rights; to exercise with order and justice those he retains, to choose with discretion the fiduciary of those he delegates, and to notice their conduct with diligence, with candor and judgement, and in general, to observe with intelligence and faithfulness all the social relations under which he shall be placed.[1]

We will not try to improve on Jefferson's vision of the purpose of American education. However, it does embrace the academic and vocational interests of the individual, and it defines the foundations of a free society.

CLUES TO THE FUTURE OF EDUCATION AND TECHNOLOGY'S ROLE

In trying to decide whether to write about possible futures for K–12 schools and their uses of IT, we first had to decide where to look for possibilities. The paths that other institutions have taken seem to offer an opportunity to document how they were impacted and why. K–12 education has features that are unique to its history, tradition, and mission that set it apart from other institutions. What has been effective for one type of organization may not be appropriate for something as large and complex as K–12 education. Nevertheless, we decided to look at the way others have integrated and responded to IT, if only to show why the response by K–12 education is different.

Some colleagues argue that the challenge of educating people for success in the modern world is fundamentally different from the undertakings of government, business, or the military. They hold that in looking outside for guidance we risk missing the real opportunities that technology presents to the profession, opportunities to deal with the unique requirements of education. They do not disagree, however, that IT can help to bring schools to levels of productivity and relevance needed to help maintain the quality of life that Americans enjoy and view as their birthright. Several people have suggested that other indicators of the future of education technology lie in the trends already showing up in so-called cutting-edge schools and districts. In the final analysis, we will try to use both approaches as we consider the next two decades of technology in education.

K–12 education presents unique challenges to anyone or anything that proposes to change its fundamental structure or its traditional culture and processes. As an institution, it is not fully understood by its critics or by its practitioners. Though K–12 schools in one community closely resemble those in others, they are local in their operation and maintenance. K–12 schools serve many purposes beyond academic learning, and, as such, they have social values that are not always considered when school reform is discussed. As we understand and recognize these values and functions better, their consideration is very likely to temper the way that individual communities decide to use IT in their K–12 schools in the coming decades.

We set the focus for our analysis at the relatively short period between 2001 and 2021. Twenty years is a long time in terms of technological change. To attempt a longer view would mean ignoring the influence of factors that are beyond our view and ability to anticipate. Even looking at the relatively short period of two decades assumes continuity on many fronts, both technological and social. If the past has taught us anything, it is the peril of assuming anything about how technology will develop or how society will use it. We have broken this twenty-year period into three roughly equal periods. Our reasoning is that these time periods represent the time needed for certain advances of the technology and also for schools and the general society to adopt them. Looking back from 2021, the biggest miss in our efforts with this book to define a future for technology in education may be when specific events actually transpire. Both technology and education have confounded their critics and forecasters sometimes by moving too slow and other times by leapfrogging steps that once seemed necessary and inevitable.

We wanted to write the book because we feel that not enough attention is being paid to some of the strategic issues surrounding technology in education. Many groups (most notably politicians at election time) have expounded on the need for more technology in schools. Critics of past and present efforts to infuse technology claim that the money has been misspent and schools are receiving little benefit from the large sums invested. "Spend less on hardware and software and more on training" is a common plea. Teacher training is the rallying cry at the turn of the century. If you come to this volume looking for previews of neat new devices and technologies, then you may be disappointed. We will look at those issues and those technologies that contain a sizeable piece of what it will take for education to redefine itself to fit the needs of the twenty-first century.

The IT industry itself learned the value of evangelizing the value of IT to schools, and it has never restrained its use of hyperbole to promote the adoption and use of its products. Even if all the claims are valid, such promotions are, ultimately, self-serving. It is obvious, even to the casual observer, that hardware and software industries view K–12 education as one of the largest markets for its products. It is also a given that profit, not improving the system, is the primary motive for the industry's support of technology in education.

Society has not addressed the issue about which direction it wants technology to take K–12 education. In this sense, K–12 education finds itself in the same position as the business community did when desktop computers began a slow trickle to the desktops of managers and employees. It looked like a good idea, but it took more than two decades before the technology had a significant impact on productivity in those sectors. Few anticipated in the early years that the very nature of business itself would be turned inside out and upside down before substantial gains in productivity were realized, a process that continues at a rapid pace today. In the end, information technologies will have a similar transformative impact on K–12 education. Many futures are possible, given what people have learned to do with IT.

From the beginning, the private sector has been engaged in an intense dialogue about how IT could and should be used. With a constant eye on the bottom line, and the ever present need to be competitive, the introduction of technology was analyzed from every angle, most notably as it impacted profit. Today, the discussion of IT in education quickly turns to the single issue of how to get more of it into schools or how to best connect schools to the Web rather than focusing on what we want K–12 schools to become in the face of the kind of restructuring that IT is driving across society.

It is generally assumed and desired that schools as we know them will and should continue in their present form. The implication for information technologies is that they will best serve by facilitating improvements in the system as it now exists. The motto of the IT industry has become "supplement not supplant" traditional education. If the lessons to be learned from others are relevant at all, these are dangerous assumptions. In the world of commerce, whether desired or not, once information technologies arrived on the scene, the advantages they gave those who used them mandated that others become adept at IT use or face extinction. For K–12 education the issue may well be whether it can embrace IT and retain its traditional character and range of services to society. Supplementing traditional schooling with IT resources may be the desire, but the result of embracing IT may inevitably lead to something entirely new and unanticipated. In the end, we may not like everything the transformation brings, and there is no guarantee that the new institution of K–12 education that results will be more effective than what we have now.

In the beginning, it is important to note one major difference between the forces that have transformed business and industry and what now faces K–12 education. *Today's technologies are more mature, more powerful, more pervasive, and more integrated than those that initially transformed the private sector.* Further, they are evolving and integrating at ever increasing speeds. All of this suggests a potential for deep structural changes for education and society in the future.

To understand how IT has transformed the world to the degree that it already has requires some understanding of the "core" features of the technologies. We are often asked the question, "When will we reach an end point in the evolution of IT?" The answer depends partly on the science behind the technology. To understand the limits and potential of technology, one has to know something about the core sciences underlying digital information technology. It is not so much what IT is today but, rather, what it is becoming that has ramifications about its impact on education. We will look only briefly at that science. The need to understand IT in order to understand where it is taking us implies that changes are also needed in what is taught in schools. Should fluency in IT, as some suggest, become a new requirement for basic literacy? If the answer is yes, then that fact alone will flavor the way it is adopted and used in K–12 education in both the short- and the midterm future.

OVERVIEW OF THE BOOK

Chapter 1 examines fundamental features of information technologies to help the reader understand the potential and limits of IT. We also examine some of the factors inherent in the technologies that presently limit their adoption and use in educational settings. We limit this discussion to three "core" technologies: computer hardware, computer software, and network connectivity.

Chapter 2 looks at the cycles of adoption and continued development of these core elements in the private sector and then compares this history to what happened in K–12 education during the early 1980s, when microcomputers first appeared in significant numbers in K–12 schools. If there are features of the technologies that are common to the needs of diverse groups such as the nation's military and its retail industry, it is likely that these same features are those that have the most potential to impact education.

Chapter 3 examines the perspective of educators on information technologies and reviews how schools have tried to use them to date. We also discuss some of the misconceptions about the requirements to successfully integrate IT into K–12 schooling.

Chapter 4 outlines challenges that K–12 education presents to the IT industry as it tries to establish a beachhead in what will be perhaps one of the largest markets for its products and services. In 1998, K–12 education operated on a budget of more than $330 billion. On the surface, at least, that is a huge potential market. The limited penetration of IT into schooling suggests that the challenges there are more than the industry has anticipated or understood. This chapter also looks at obstacles that have prevented K–12 schools, both public and private, from being more proactive in the adoption and use of technology. Obstacles exist, and new ones are encountered regularly. Some are inherent in the logistics and politics of education, and others belong to the nature of the technologies themselves as they have evolved.

Chapter 5 offers our view of how present technologies will fare in the near-term future or the years between 2001 and 2007. Critics of education and the IT industry itself are making very strong claims for new devices, new services, and integration strategies. Which will survive the shakeout that will occur during this period?

Chapter 6 looks at the midterm future that covers the years 2008–14. We consider many of the hot topic strategies and tools schools will take into this period and suggest which will have lasting impact and which will not. This will also be a time of consolidation as the most promising technologies reach maturity and as the capabilities and understanding of K–12 educators reach the point that they could begin a process that will create an effective system of providing learning services for the twenty-first century.

Chapter 7 attempts to describe the transformation most likely to occur in K–12 education during the third period, the long-term future that covers 2014 through 2021. Chapter 8 takes a brief look at what we call the social value of K–12 education in its present form and asks what will have to be retained by any new system that will replace it. Finally, the epilogue looks at the question of what some of the unrecognized social values of public education as it has evolved in the twentieth century are and examines the risk that much of that value could be lost in the transformation brought about by IT.

NOTE

1. Thomas Jefferson, Report of the Commissioners for the University of Virginia, August 4, 1818 (the Rector and Visitors of the University of Virginia, 1995). Available at http://etext.lib.virginia.edu.

1

Engines of Change

In 1970 Alvin Toffler, in his book *Future Shock,*[1] asked whether the human race could survive what he called *future shock,* his term for the impact people were beginning to feel from the effects of accelerating rates of social and technological change. The answer, as evidenced by our presence here thirty years later, is, "Yes, of course we can adapt, and we can do so at rates no one dreamed possible as recently as forty years ago." Having experienced societal transformations driven by technologies such as the printing press, electricity, the electric motor, and the automobile, people today are curious about how a new generation of technologies will impact them. Information technology, or IT, is at the forefront of that concern. Our curiosity embraces a need to visualize the positive benefits of change and reflects our instinct to look for its downside. The experiences of the past are not forgotten, and they include the fact that earlier transformations brought problems and pains along with the benefits. Educators are no exception in their need to know. Indeed, educators have witnessed what the power of IT and related fields can do in other settings. It is in the field of education that information technologies have yet to wreak their full effects.

EDUCATIONAL TECHNOLOGY VERSUS
INFORMATION TECHNOLOGY

Immediately, when discussing technology in education, people tend to think of computers, specifically the desktop computer. In reality, technology in education embraces many technologies and many processes. It is more productive to the use the broader term *information technology,* or *IT,* when discussing technology and society or technology and schools. The broader field of IT lies at the heart of the revolution sweeping old institutions away and is in the process of transforming K–12 education as well. The computer by itself was never up to the task.

The term *educational technology* is frequently used to denote programs and systems designed specifically to teach this or that subject or concept. Educational technology, as such, is usually viewed as a discrete subset of the domain of IT. For example, various companies produce integrated learning systems, sometimes referred to as ILS. Integrated learning systems purport to deliver instruction in a subject that is individualized to a single student's needs and then test the student's progress or mastery of a unit or "frame" of instruction before going to the next. This approach is an extension of an older process called programmed learning and uses the computer to present and manage the process. This is not the educational technology that is considered in this book. Rather, technology in education is the same as technology in business or industry. It is the total range of IT and its impact on public and private K–12 education that is our subject.

Business, industry, government, and the military have their versions of technologies that "teach." Training systems and simulators are common in these fields. However, it has not been training technologies that have been at the root of the change that IT has brought to these organizations. Rather, it was how and where information technologies were applied to fundamental processes of organizations that fueled their "restructuring" or "reengineering." The impact of technology on education between 2001 and 2021 will result from these same primary sources and processes. The rate at which educators learn to make IT applications and IT-enabled processes fundamental to their enterprise will be a primary factor in how swiftly technology changes K–12 education. This premise supports our belief that educators must learn from the mistakes and successes of others. The most significant impact of IT on K–12 education is not likely to come from digitized curriculum content and its delivery via classroom computers. On the other hand, this is precisely where federal and state governments have tried to provide catalysts for technology integration into K–12 education. Not only does this emphasis not help the transfer of technology to education, it also diverts attention away from core processes that most need attention.

THE PAST AS PROLOGUE

Since the development of language, humankind has had an information technology at its disposal. In its time, the invention of the printing press was a quantum leap in the advancement of IT. The impact of the printing press on human history is well documented. Just as the printing press transformed society, in the century just past, the development of digital processing around the computer ushered in our present digital version of IT. Our generation has witnessed the impact of IT on business, government, the military, and to an increasing degree, the personal lives of individuals.

To put into perspective the short history of digital IT, and to suggest its future impact on education and society, consider how IT has evolved and been applied since the early 1940s (see table 1.1). Note shifts in the areas impacted as technologies mature and as new components are introduced.

Information Technology Concepts and Elements

A semantic differential (or language barrier) impedes the national dialogue about technology and society. This is true even within the field of

Table 1.1. Time Line for Computer Development

Period	Stage	Description
1940–69	Dawn of the computer age	Large corporations and governments were impacted significantly once they learned how to use the power of information technology to organize, store, retrieve, and manipulate data.
1970–90	Introduction of the personal computer	Smaller organizations and the common person were empowered just as big business and government had been by the "big iron" of the 1950s and 1960s.
1990–2000	The decade of the computer network	Computers around the globe are connected to one another and a new age of communications is launched.
2000–10	Personal computers and networks mature and become pervasive and invisible	Fundamental changes in human communications modes and interactions result. All are impacted.
2011–20	Computer applications evolve quickly as hardware and communication standards are both stabilized and globalized	The form and shape of the first stage of digital culture are established. Networked computer communications are essential to most if not all human endeavors in the fields of commerce, business, science, art, entertainment, and education.

IT, for terms and concepts are used interchangeably. This is not uncommon in new fields. Digital IT represents the integration of knowledge and concepts from traditional disciplines and others from newly emerging fields of study. This helps explain differences in how terms are used and why different terms are sometimes used for the same concept or process. To foster understanding, we offer the following review of essential terms and concepts as part of a short history of digital information technology.

The Domain of Information Technology

Information technology as a field of study embraces applications from physics, chemistry, mathematics, logic, language, and the relatively new field of information science. From physics and chemistry, we have learned how to create electrical components that reliably repeat operations that represent physical, electrical states of being. For example, given a precise set of conditions, an electrical pulse will be present or absent at a particular place on a device called an integrated circuit. That binary condition (electricity present or electricity absent) forms the basis of electronic computing today. These electrical states (present or absent) are symbolically represented using base 2 arithmetic (base 2 uses two digits, 0–1, compared with base 10 arithmetic, which uses ten digits, 0–9). Two digits, 0 and 1, define the foundation of computing processes, hence the terms *digital information technology, the digital age,* and so forth. Individual digits are referred to as *bits,* short for "binary digits." Everything that computers do can be represented digitally using patterns of electrical states symbolically represented by two-digit code.

Given digital processing capabilities of integrated circuits, we use logic to define rules about how microelectrical components (switches) on these circuits behave given the presence or absence of certain patterns of electrical pulses. In a simple example, IF/THEN logic can be used to control a device: IF a particular pattern of pulses and absence of pulses exists, THEN the processor displays a particular alphanumeric character on a screen.

As the power of chips to process digital pulses has improved over time, computer scientists have developed higher levels of computer "languages" to create these patterns of "pulse/no pulse." In the beginning, each pattern of four or eight bits was created manually by setting a bank of switches to off or on positions and then transmitting that pattern to the processor. A transmission is called an instruction. Today, advances in programming languages enable the use of human language to create complex sets of instructions. This makes it easier and more cost effective to create complex applications to run on high-speed computer systems. The domain of IT embraces computer languages and the software applications that are created with them. Early languages include BASIC, COBOL, and FOR-

TRAN. Today, we use languages with names like C, VISUAL BASIC, or JAVA. A large part of the digital IT revolution is tied to the increasing efficiency of computer languages to transmit instructions to the processor on integrated circuits. The continued evolution of computer language will be a contributing factor to the domain of IT each step of the way toward 2020.

Just as English has emerged as the language of the Internet and has enabled a global e-commerce phenomenon, the emergence of a standard high-level language for computer programming will facilitate the development of new and more complex software. The IT industry has come to understand the power of standards, and the evolution of a standard programming language is likely within the next ten years. Programs or applications are developed and refined regularly by the likes of companies such as Oracle, Microsoft, and Apple. It is relatively easy to represent different types of information in digital form. Text, sound, and visual information can all be represented digitally. Out of this ability comes the term *multimedia,* which really describes the merger of text, image, and sound into one medium of storage. The movement of our stored archive of information from media such as print, tape, and film (all analog technologies) to digitally based media such as discs and arrays of computer memory chips has initiated what some call the process of "digital fusion," a process by which all types of information (sound, text, and visual) take on digital form. In digital form, information acquires new or added value as it is used and manipulated. The fact that someone has used an item adds more information about that particular piece of information, that is, its usefulness to someone. This new class of information about information represents added value in databases. Data *about* data are called metadata.

In digital form, information can be more quickly manipulated as well as more efficiently stored and retrieved. This characteristic of digital information has led to new fields of endeavor that are dedicated to developing efficient models or designs of information collections and to developing standards and techniques for handling information. Information systems have formed the basis for entirely new fields of study in universities. Career fields in information science are rapidly expanding in nature as they also increase in availability, especially in areas that deal with information architectures or protocols for the exchange and transfer of information from point to point.

The ability to digitally store, retrieve, and manipulate text, images, and sound has created the need for high-speed and reliable transport and connectivity tools to enable people to access and use the information. Copper-wire and fiber-optic cable now vie with infrared and radio waves to become the ultimate transport media (broadband, or high capacity, as opposed to "baseband," or lower capacity). Computer networking began with coaxial cable connections among computers and printers in local offices and buildings and has evolved into regional, national, and global networks of connections of many types. Networking reaches its most elaborate expression in the form of today's Internet. The Internet is a complex "web" of smaller, connected networks spread around the world, and they and the Internet are expanding at rates unparalleled in human history.

Advancements in IT foundation areas will affect both the degree and the rate of change we experience in education and society. What happens within three primary foundation areas of IT will be most influential in shaping the future of IT. These are hardware, software, and the network connections and protocols that allow communications from one computer to another.

HARDWARE: THE CENTRAL PROCESSING UNIT

The central processing unit (CPU) or integrated circuit is the actual digital computer in a computer system, not the box that sits on one's desk or lap. This processor chip controls or processes all the pieces of information (bits) that flow within a particular computer system. Processors have evolved since their early introduction in a variety of ways, and their evolution is making them both more powerful and cheaper. The evolution of central processor chips is based on improving their design and packing more features (switches) onto the chip. Other design features include developing more efficient layouts of components on the chip to shorten the distances that bits have to travel and the use of materials and processes that improve the rate at which the processor can transmit its bits of information. Early microcomputers processed information eight bits at a time (a bit stream of eight logical 0s and 1s), and today's high-end processors gulp information sixty-four bits at a time. The more bits a processor can handle in a single operation, the faster the processor is. Speed is a major component of the processor's "power."

The manufacture of these processors is a highly competitive business. Different companies have different chip architectures around which they build their designs. We commonly hear of Motorola and Intel "chipsets" or chip architectures. We speak of these as we speak of the engines in our automobiles. Indeed, they are the engines of IT devices.

The 0.1 Barrier

An obvious question to ask about the future of processor chips is whether the science behind the design and manufacture of semiconductor devices can continue to make them infinitely more powerful. The answer is no. The laws of quantum physics place physical limits on what can be etched onto the surface of a semiconductor to produce microprocessors. We can only get "more" onto the processor by making the components smaller and the chip more compact. Smaller chips mean that the electrons have less distance to travel from switch to switch and that the manufacturer can get more chips out of a single wafer of semiconductor material. Science has been enabling the production of smaller and smaller circuits on semiconductor material. However, at the 0.1 micron level that process reaches the physical limits imposed by quantum physics. At the 0.1 micron level things are as small and as close together as they can get, and the evolution of microprocessors built around semiconductor technology ends at that point.

Based on a concept called Moore's Law, it is estimated that such a limit will be reached no later than 2020—perhaps sooner. Moore's Law is based on microprocessor evolution over a number of years and shows that the power of processors doubles every eighteen months or so without any increase in price. At that rate, our present microprocessors will double in power about thirteen times by 2020. Beyond 2020, a new technology, something other than semiconductor-based processing units, will need to be used if digital IT is to evolve further. No one can say whether such a technology will be on hand at the time, but the odds are that such a technology is already in the incubator, perhaps one of the hybrid electro-optical techniques in testing. Optical processors use light rather than electricity as the basis for processing. Hybrid electro-optical devices use a combination of both.

Even though semiconductors reach a theoretical end to their evolution in the not-too-distant future, it is a safe bet that information technologies will continue to evolve beyond that point. The economic forces driving their evolution are themselves not likely to abate. Even if development should come to an end with the 0.1 barrier, the mature semiconductor processor will have increased in processing capability by a factor of thirteen.

It is difficult to imagine the kinds of applications that such processors will enable. One fact is clear, however. The technology that does transform education will be a more mature and a more powerful technology than the one that has changed other institutions. At the same time, it will be more pervasive and, one would assume, more versatile. All these suggest the potential for sweeping changes in how people learn in our society by 2020 regardless of how the 0.1 barrier problem is solved.

Beyond Speed

Features of integrated circuits other than processing power need to be considered to understand their potential impact on education. These are cost and the invisibility factor. From the beginning, the trend has been for dramatic decreases in the cost of integrated circuits from one generation to the next. Today, microchips are viewed as commodities like grain, pork, or beef. The day is near when the price of an individual chip will be less than one cent—less than the cost of a piece of printer paper. At that price, devices can be developed that are single purpose and single use in their design and application. Disposable computer devices in the future are a real possibility.

The cost of IT resources has been a factor inhibiting their adoption by K–12 education. K–12 education has been struggling to develop and maintain a critical mass of information technology to enable broad integration. Even though the cost has been coming down steadily, and today's entry-level classroom computer costs about one-half less than the personal computer of the late 1980s, the size and scope of K–12 education continues to make integrating IT extremely expensive for schools. Fully functional computers still cost several hundred dollars each, and it does not help that their useful life is becoming shorter and shorter. Mass production of very cheap single-use devices, however, will help overcome this obstacle. When devices fall into the $200.00 range, more schools will begin to consider a one-to-one ratio of computers to students.

Looking at the development of the computer market since 1980, it seems reasonable to expect that the price of IT components will reach a level at which they can be widely deployed in K–12 education by 2005. "Widely deployed" means that each learner in the system will probably have multiple devices at his or her disposal for personal use. Whereas today we count ratios of students to one computer, we very well may be counting the number of computing devices to one student as soon as 2007.

The Invisibility Factor

We should avoid the temptation to look at the future in terms of the present level and type of technology. Just as electricity and electric motors were integrated into other devices and became "invisible," IT devices will become more attached to other things. Much has already happened in this respect. As the recent Y2K problem revealed, embedded chips are everywhere. Telephones, televisions, cars, planes, kitchen appliances, manufacturing tools, implements of war and antiwar (a term introduced by Alvin Toffler in his book *War and Anti-War*)[2] teem with control devices built around the microcomputer chip. The field of nanotechnology (the design and manufacture of very small machines using microchips) is advancing rapidly. It is not unreasonable to expect that these miniature, "smart" devices will be assimilated by older technologies and, as the transhumanists argue, even by human beings themselves.

The CPU represents the fundamental tool of the digital age, akin to moveable type in the age of Gutenberg. In summary, electronic microprocessor chips will probably end their evolutionary path around 2020, to be replaced with technologies not yet identified. In the process of getting there, processors will become more than thirteen times more powerful, their cost will be reduced to almost nothing, and their size will approach the microscopic. Each of these features will remove barriers to the full integration of technology in education.

SOFTWARE: FUELING THE ENGINES

In the previous section we looked at the primary hardware component of IT devices, the CPU, and considered how it has and likely will evolve. The second major domain of IT, in our view, is software. We refer to computer programs as *software*. Software, or computer programs, are simply sets of instructions for the CPU to carry out. They have no real physical existence other than the magnetic, optical, or electrical medium that contains them; hence they are "soft." Patterns represented logically by 0s and 1s form the physical existence of software. Originally, instructions were created by setting switches to on or off positions and were transmitted to the CPU one at a time. This was cumbersome to say the least. Then we learned how to translate instruction sets into other mathematical systems so that they can be stored and reused any time a particular instruction needs to be executed.

Very early, from the 1940s through the 1950s, the binary system of "hole" or "no hole" in strips of paper or "punch cards" was used to contain and transfer instructions to computer circuits. Later we learned to represent binary digits as magnetic states, positive or negative charges of tiny particles of iron oxide coated onto a plastic disk or tape. Magnetic tape and then magnetic disks enabled program developers to store increasingly large and complex instruction sets. We continue to find innovative ways to represent binary states, and each innovation increases the storage capacity of computing systems and improves the speed at which the CPU can access and "read" the instructions. CD-ROM represents an optically based binary system of small indentations or lack of indentations on a reflective plastic disc. Each stage of the evolution of storage devices has increased both the capacity to store and the speed of access to the information that the devices contain.

When it comes to software, however, other factors are more influential on its evolution than how it is physically represented and stored. It is necessary to distinguish between the different kinds of software that computing systems use.

Operating Systems

System software, sometimes called an operating system, or OS, is designed to enable the CPU to communicate with other devices that are attached to the main logic board. The first device we needed to attach was a disk drive; hence, early operating systems alluded to the disk operating function (DOS). TRSDOS and MSDOS are early examples. System software resides on an external storage device (CD, or hard drive) and is loaded into the computer system's internal memory, or Random Access Memory (RAM). In RAM, the operating system enables the CPU to manage, receive, and execute instructions from other application software. System software combines with the processing power of the CPU to do a task faster, more accurately, or more efficiently than it could be done otherwise. System software has evolved from proprietary programs written for individual machines to what will eventually emerge as a universal standard for operating instructions in computing devices. Today we have operating systems from Microsoft, from Sun, and from Apple Computer, among others. A relatively new entry on the scene, Linux, is a new version of an old system called UNIX, and it is becoming widely adopted.

The future of technology in education and elsewhere will be driven in part by system software developments. The future of these systems is clouded by the probability of the breakup of Microsoft by the U.S. Justice Department after its successful suit in federal court in 2000. If supported in the appeals process, the breakup may either impede the development of a standard operating system or facilitate it. Only time will tell. When any computer can talk to and run the software designed for any other, we will finally have achieved interoperability among computers and software, and another obstacle to the adoption and use of IT in education will have fallen. The Internet has been remarkable in driving Internet protocols across many dimensions of IT, and it is rapidly setting standards for software development and transmission of digital material from point to point. Some feel that the continued development of the Internet will ultimately lead to universal standards for software development and information architectures.

System software depends on an abundance of memory chips and faster CPUs for its evolution, and as we have seen, those elements continue to improve and come down in price. Another factor that influences software development relates to how K–12 institutions adopt and use technologies. The pressure on developers today is for more reliable and user-friendly software tools and hardware devices. In the future, as education embraces IT more completely, the pressure will be to create more complete sets of tools that can facilitate the complex functions of teaching, learning, and managing schools and districts. This is the same pattern observed in business and industry throughout the 1980s and 1990s.

Application Software

Application programs represent a second major category of software. Application software today is created for a particular operating system and works in tandem with the CPU to execute sets of instructions. For example, by clicking on a particular icon in Microsoft Word using my Macintosh computer, I send a set of instructions to the CPU to arrange the text of a paragraph into double line spacing. The instruction is executed instantly, and the text appears as I wish. Early word-processing applications required a string of commands at the beginning of the block of text and a string of commands at the end of the block to be set. The graphical user interface that makes computing easier today is enabled by the evolution of the CPU, higher capacity and cheaper memory, more capable and efficient operating systems, and the evolution of individual application packages such as WordPerfect or Microsoft Word.

Application software for K–12 education is in its infancy. Schools have adopted many of the tools (productivity software) used by everyone else. But fully integrated application suites that can enhance the primary business of education remain to be defined.

Software Development Approaches

Changes in how software is developed will help shape the future of technology in education. Today, most software used in education is "off-the-shelf" software. These are packages developed for common use. They run on a particular type of CPU and with a particular operating system. Thousands of such programs now offer instruction in most areas of the school curriculum. Other widely used applications include personal productivity packages such as word-processing, database, and spreadsheet applications. Off-the-shelf software works the same for everyone. Its capabilities and limitations are the same for everyone. Being mass produced, off-the-shelf software is relatively inexpensive. The large investments that developers must make in such software can be recovered quickly in the mass market.

Custom software, on the other hand, used to dominate computing in the days before the desktop computer, was written for specific applications and specific settings. Custom software more precisely met the needs of the organization developing it. A major advantage of custom software was that it did not require a business to adjust its practices or procedures to accommodate the software. As the microcomputer achieved dominance, more and more applications moved to off-the-shelf varieties whereby one package dealt with a broad range of standard or common business practices. A major disadvantage of off-the-shelf software is that it does not meet all the needs of anyone.

With off-the-shelf applications customers have two choices: (1) modify their business practices around the software's capabilities or (2) have someone "tweak" the standard package to achieve a better fit with their businesses. Neither approach affords quite the same level of usefulness as custom software does, but both are cheaper than custom development. Custom software design and production requires skills in fields such as analysis, data modeling, data architecture, and computer interfacing. As such, developing custom software is usually cost prohibitive for most school applications.

Schools represent unique communities and organizations, and, like businesses, they share many of the same processes and needs. While off-the-shelf software can meet some needs of schools, customized or customizable software is needed as well. The lack of software designed to meet the special needs of schools as institutions and learners as individuals has limited the adoption of IT in education. Trends in software design, standards, and programming tools such as computer-assisted software engineering tools will help reduce the cost of bringing more custom software to education. In other words, we are learning to use the computer to help us efficiently produce computer application software. At the same time, the decreasing cost of memory devices and their increasing storage capacity are enabling more complex applications to run on cheaper desktop computers. Finally, faster, more powerful CPUs are enabling the computer system to execute these complex instruction sets at speeds that make them increasingly attractive.

However, there are other factors that inhibit the development of software applications for education. Software development is labor intensive. For example, a recent custom application developed for a school district's special education department required more than 2,000 man-hours to produce it. The software company that wrote the application charged an average of $90.00 per man-hour. That brought the cost of the application to more than $225,000—a large sticker price indeed, but the district determined that the efficiency it gained in processing eligibility studies and developing individualized education plans for students would offset the cost of custom software development.

The initial cost of developing such a package was such that the software company was unwilling to bring this piece of software to market. It was not sure that there was a market beyond the district that wanted the software originally. There was no guarantee that other districts would have needs similar enough to make the program useful to them. Consequently, the district that wanted the custom package had to bear the full cost of its development. In the end, the application did prove useful to other districts in the state, and several bought it. Such an outcome is an exception rather than the rule. Bringing any piece of software to market is a risky venture. Tens of thousands of man-hours would be wasted if a product did not meet a wide need and also become widely accepted.

Software companies look at what are called vertical markets for the programs they develop. Banking, for example, is a vertical market. Within banking, the programs that manage ATM transactions represent a more specialized vertical market. In these cases, a need is widespread, and the market for ATM management software is considered strong. So companies are willing to invest time and money to compete for a piece of that market.

Education represents a "fractured" market to software developers. K–12 education in particular supports multiple computing platforms, more so than most other organizations. The Macintosh OS competes with Microsoft and others for the education market. Developers must write for smaller segments of the total education market or invest more heavily in developing simultaneously for both segments and the whole market. Multiple platforms fracture the market and reduce its attractiveness to developers, and, as a consequence, many potentially useful applications have not been developed at all.

Standards for applications are common in other, established vertical markets. Standards for data exchange among databases, for example, have been developed by professional and industry committees that create and maintain standards. Proprietary programs, common to the age of mainframe computing, that worked on only one platform or manufacturer's line of equipment are disappearing. Open systems and standardized approaches are the key to success beyond 2000.

Until recently, however, little attention has been given to standards for applications developed for the education market. A new initiative, the School Interoperability Framework, promises to start education down a path that the private sector has already traveled. K–12 applications have usually stood alone and have had limited ability to share data or interact with one another. This not only further fractures the education software market but also limits the range of applications that educators can make of the software that is available. For example, a package to manage cafeteria receipts will not integrate with a package to manage student grades because they are designed and developed differently without thought of integrating them into a common architecture. Consequently, it is common to find schools running many different computing systems (on different networks) and replicating data entry and data management procedures. It is common to find separate systems for food services, library management, student record management, budget, finance, transportation, research and planning, instructional support and planning, and so on in a single district administration center. Redundant and sometimes conflicting systems complicate IT adoption and reduce its attractiveness to end users. Chapter 5 looks at the role of standards in more depth.

A major advance in the use of digital information technologies in the private sector has been the development of data warehouses and data marts. These collections of information generated about an organization's business products and processes fully integrate everything that is known about the enterprise and its products or services. Making such data available to all desktops on the organization's network informs decision making about virtually any dimension of the business. Scientific management takes a major leap forward when fully integrated data warehouses and analysis tools are employed. The complexity of K–12 education is such that it should be a logical candidate for decision support systems. In fact, much data are still collected and analyzed manually.

In the private sector, some companies have gone even farther and created information architectures that integrate their data with those of their suppliers and customers. Superstores such as Wal-Mart, for example, let suppliers access their inventory database on a day-to-day basis so that stock never runs out and gets delivered "just in time." Point-of-sale computer terminals (cash registers of old) collect information about products that are sold and about who bought them. The bar codes and high-speed bar code scanner supply data about each transaction. Those data are carefully analyzed and compared with other data as the marketing and manufacturing process learns to adjust to consumer tastes and trends. The process of collecting and using such comprehensive data is called value-added computing, and it has revolutionized the way in which businesses and organizations interact with one another and their constituencies.

K–12 education has much to learn from business and military applications of IT. Change there has been brought about not so much by the creation of powerful new application programs as by the way that standard communication and database tools have been applied in innovative ways. Educators, too, in time will learn to use such tools with their fundamental or core processes. The result will bring major changes to K–12 education. Cutting-edge school districts are already creating data warehouses and learning how best to use them. At the 1999 and 2000 meetings of the National School Board's Institute for the Transfer of Technology to Education, data warehouses were discussed in several sessions, and dozens of vendors had exhibits that offered data warehouse development services.

Another dimension of software that will have major impact on K–12 education relates to the content of the curriculum. This is the information that traditionally resides in textbooks, libraries, and reference books. The digital revolution has already touched this dimension of K–12 education in a significant way. With the Internet increasing its reach into K–12 classrooms, it is now possible to teach and learn without textbooks. On-line information resources and large collections of periodicals and articles on networked CD-ROM towers all vastly expanded the resource base for teaching and learning. On-line virtual libraries are supplementing traditional libraries at an increasing pace and are beginning to supplant them in some cases. School library and media centers, as traditionally defined, are likely to be among the first casualties in the coming K–12 transformation, as virtual libraries and virtual learning centers reach their mature form.

CONNECTIVITY: THE AGE OF
NETWORKS AND INTERNETWORKS

From the discussion of hardware and software above, it begins to become apparent that in the field of IT, different technologies are woven into a tight interdependency to create capabilities any one could not support. The CPU cannot do much without access to its dynamic memory chips or the operating instructions it places there. The operating system itself has limited functionality and does not give the end user everything needed to deal with a specific task. Application software and other devices attached to the CPU are needed to do "useful" things.

It was when computers were connected to other computers or "networked" that the capacity of IT took its next quantum leap forward. In the beginning, networking allowed different computers to share devices such as printers, plotters, or modems for communication. Sharing these peripheral devices meant that the business could "leverage" investments in them and achieve a greater return on those investments. A device such as a laser printer is productive only when it is used. The more users that are connected to it via some networking strategy, the more it is used and the greater the return is on the investment made in it. Sharing also leverages the device in the sense that every desktop with a computer does not need its own printer, modem, or high-capacity hard drive for storage or backup. Sharing peripherals probably initiated the development of the first networks for desktop computers.

It was not long, however, before users discovered another category of sharing that improved business practice. Information sharing immediately began to produce benefits for organizations. Centralized and special computers called file servers were added to local area networks (local connections among computers and devices) so that documents could be readily shared and available anywhere one could get connected to the file server. Instant availability of documents, sharing and working on the same document from remote locations, and letting others in the organization work on or add new value to a document or data collection are all practices that ignited the "knowledge-value" revolution.

As user demand grew, new technologies had to be developed to support larger and larger networks. So great were the benefits to organizations of instant communications and access to shared data that some private networks became global in scope. Banks, along with some retail and manufacturing institutions, very early gained significant advantages in their marketplace because of their value-added, networked IT resources and practices. By the early 1980s, one had to be networked and achieving higher and higher efficiencies and levels of productivity in order to stay in business. The great economic boom in the United States during the 1990s can be tied directly to the improvement in productivity that has been fueling the U.S. and global economy for more than ten years.

The U.S. military also recognized the value of information to the art and practice of war and national defense. The Defense Advanced Research Projects Administration spent tremendous sums to build networks and developed network protocols to support the U.S. military during the Cold War. It was out of these efforts that today's Internet was born. For a full history of the Internet visit the Internet Society's website at http://www.isoc.org/internet/history.

Networking strategies, like CPUs, operating systems, and application programs, began as proprietary products and services. For some time each was developed and supported by a single vendor. IBM with its proprietary Token Ring networking architecture at one time seemed destined to become the universal standard for networks. It was the development of the Open Systems Interconnection standard that paved the way for a more open and competitive environment. These standards created efficient communication protocols for all the devices and levels within networks.

Once standards were developed for networking and became widely adopted, individual networks could be combined into internetworks. Standards meant that all the devices were speaking the same language. The larger the network, the greater the value added to the information available on the network. It was out of such networks that the Information Age was born. Computers plus networks enabled digital information to become the raw material for the global economy long before the year 2000.

How networks evolve in terms of standards, delivery media (copper wire, fiber, radio, etc.), switching and routing techniques, and something called compression algorithms will influence educational applications between now and 2020. The real value of technology in K–12 education did not become apparent until the capability of networked computers was realized. Access to vast collections of information, direct access to experts in the field, and the ability to collaborate within learning communities ignited the imagination of educators, and the rush to "wire" every classroom in the nation is now more than a decade old.

Some leading-edge districts are into a second phase of networking in the sense that they are tearing out networks they installed as recently as ten years ago. Early networks of certain designs cannot support transport of the billions of bits of information per second that are now required in a multimedia, technology-rich school environment. Network design and installation are expensive. The price for completely networking an average-sized elementary school with 600 students and 200 computers can exceed $200,000 in 2001. This does not include the cost of the computers, software, and support personnel to make it all work. As the evolution of networking technologies matures around 2010, K–12 education can move forward with infrastructures in place that can support levels of information transport capable of redefining what a school is.

Education already consumes high volumes of networked multimedia. As prices for these materials decline and they become more closely tied to school curricula, their use will replace the use of traditional textbooks and most other media. How communities connect their classrooms to one another and to the rest of the networked world will play a major role in their schedule of transformation. Chapter 2 explores this phenomenon in more detail.

In chapter 1, we have identified three core technologies that have shaped the current state of technology in education. The evolution of these same three technologies will be a major factor in the ultimate role IT will come to play in K–12 schools. All three technologies will advance significantly well before the year 2020, and by that time K–12 education will have had time to learn how to use these resources to support its goals and objectives. Undoubtedly, different communities will have different schedules and will take different paths in the transformation of their schools, but by 2020 the information revolution will have brought tremendous change to how K–12 education is designed and delivered in the United States.

Three trends have characterized the personal computer from its inception and will continue for the foreseeable future. First, computers will continue to get smaller until they reach the point at which they can be easily assimilated into even the smallest devices and attached to clothing and other prosthetics commonly used by humans. New devices that are not so common will be enabled by microdevices. Second, computing devices will become increasingly functional. Functionality gains will be based on increasing the processing speed and power of the integrated circuit itself and on the ability of humans to develop efficient and reliable software applications to take advantage of more speed and power. Finally, microdevices will continue to become more affordable. All three trends will contribute to the technology becoming pervasive across many dimensions of our lives and our world.

NOTES

1. Alvin Toffler, *Future Shock* (New York: Bantam Books, 1970).
2. Alvin Toffler, *War and Anti-War* (New York: Warner Books, 1995).

2
Technology Adoption and Organizational Change: Lessons from the Private Sector

A brief look at how information technologies established themselves solidly in other organizations will cast light on similar processes now under way in K–12 education. The many variables that challenge IT managers in the private sector often operate similarly in K–12 education, but there are differences in the education environment that present unique challenges.

IN THE BEGINNING

Faced with increasing numbers of personal computers (PCs) appearing on employee desktops and rapidly growing departmental budget requests for them, managers in the private sector were as unprepared for the new technology as educators have been. Initial reactions to microcomputers in business and industry were not always favorable, especially within the traditional power centers of IT, the data-processing (DP) department. Those who brought PCs into organizations over the objections of DP executives usually did so with the understanding that they would be on their own and without support from DP staff. In retrospect, while it may seem that data-processing departments were acting solely to protect their domain of influence, it is also true that the IT professionals of the time were so used to centralized computing models that they could not see the potential of small, less powerful devices. Past practice, tradition, and even the culture of IT departments effectively blinded the professionals to what was taking shape right before their eyes. Though they resisted the desktop PC for some time, the networked PC effectively blew the doors off the back room and changed IT forever.

SKUNK WORKS AND ENTREPRENEURS

A combination of "skunk works" and individual entrepreneurs emerged to challenge IT traditions. A skunk works is an operation within an operation, often not officially sanctioned. In other words, someone or some group decided to think and act "outside the box." It did not take long for the success stories of some skunk works to reach mythical proportions. Among those to gain notoriety was a Lockheed group that produced the B-2 bomber. Skunk works were and are quick to use whatever tools enable them to be more effective or efficient. They quickly embraced the microcomputer and data network. Many of our most useful innovations and products have evolved from skunk works. Today many companies have attempted to formally establish skunk works or small, semi-autonomous groups within their organizations and give them a green light to innovate outside normal channels and procedures. Charter schools in the K–12 education arena may be attempts to do the same thing in public education.

EMPOWERMENT OR WHEELS FOR THE MIND

Word-processing software, spreadsheets, and, eventually, database applications began to provide users with information and resources that previously had been held inside the "big iron" of the data-processing department. The tools and techniques to retrieve information inside mainframe computers were complex and required the skills of data-processing professionals to access it after it was collected and stored. Requests for "reports" or access to data had to go through the DP staff. Not only was access controlled, but much information was never collected and stored because of the costs and complexity of managing it. Complexity and controlled access guaranteed the job security of DP professionals and the continued growth of DP within organizations.

Once "power" PC users developed proficiency with the new tools, they began to ask DP departments for data in an electronic form in which they could import it into their desktop machines and, there, manipulate it at will. Feeling the threat of independent users to their "turf," traditional data-processing departments and managers frequently fought the proliferation of PCs into their organizations. It was common in the 1980s and early 1990s to see data-processing department managers speak fearfully of supervisors who used or were learning to use PCs. Loss of control and loss of data integrity were very much on their minds. Although both fears were well founded, history shows that the benefits to organizations have far outweighed the problems of proliferating data and skilled PC users taking matters into their own hands. Users began to demonstrate the unique ability of fast-calculating machines to "leverage" their work. In a competitive workplace, this fueled the rush for others to do the same. When a person becomes more productive and more effective thorough the use of information-processing tools, the result is called empowerment.

Once networks were added to the IT mix, users literally were empowered to communicate across time and space and dramatically increase their individual and collective productivity. As the history of the great economic boom of the 1990s is written, much of the credit for its strength and longevity will be attributed to the empowerment effects of IT.

COOKING AND GROWING THE REVOLUTION

In retrospect, it seems that the computer exploded onto the scene and immediately transformed everything it touched. In fact, the process was a gradual one. Today, business, industry, government, and military organizations are ahead of education in the adoption of information technology because they started seriously integrating IT into their fundamental operations more than two decades earlier than education has. At the same time, these organizations have had to contend with competitive forces that are missing in education.

It is important for educators to note that in the early stages of adoption, the PC had a limited impact on military and private organizations. Neither the power of the PC nor its potential contribution was fully recognized until decades after its introduction. Before real change could take place, pioneering individuals and groups had to make effective use of the primitive IT tools of the time and teach the rest so that they could follow. The applications they had to work with early on were of limited use because of their simplicity and the complexity of using them. Some dedicated users persisted in the face of these shortcomings, and exciting and innovative uses for the technology were developed over time. Eventually, "killer" applications began to emerge in the private sector.

In the 1980s and 1990s, there were early adopters and groups in K–12 education. They became power users, and the progress that IT has made in K–12 schools to date can largely be attributed to their successes. However, IT has not permeated the business side of K–12 education as it has in business and industry. There are numerous reasons for this, and, as we progress toward 2020, it is possible that the obstacles endemic to K–12 schooling will be overcome and the resulting K–12 environment will be as different from the twentieth-century K–12 school as today's restructured, right-sized, and customer-oriented business is from its 1960s counterpart.

The absence of "killer" applications in K–12 education has been a drawback. K–12 schooling still struggles to find the right application, the right mix, and the right place for IT. Is it only a matter of time until killer applications will be developed for K–12 education? Consider the following killer application from the business sector and its impact.

BAR CODE SCANNERS AND THE POINT-OF-SALE TERMINAL: A KILLER APPLICATION

When some companies suddenly began to gain real advantage in the marketplace through new and innovative uses of the PC, the information revolution really started to roll. The development of the Universal Product Code (a unique number assigned to a product) and the representation of that number in a binary form, that is, a black line or absence of a black line, led to major advantages in the marketplace for those who knew how to use them. Bar codes are now ubiquitous. To understand the importance of bar codes, consider that based on the recommendation of its National Task Force on Information Technology and Software Development, the Government of India stated in its IT action plan that every product sold in India would be bar coded by 2003. You can find the Indian plan on the Web at http://it-taskforce.nic.in/.

Once everything has a unique identification number, an inexpensive, high-speed computer can collect information to a degree not previously imagined. When software to read and transmit the bar code on the product package was linked to a computer that was equipped with a scanning device to "read" the bar code, all that was needed was a way to transmit that data to a central computer where they could be used for planning and management. Analysis of the sale of an item was used to gain insight into its market and the buying habits of those who purchase it. Data networking was the missing ingredient, and once networks were available, the point-of-sale terminal was born.

Cash registers quickly gave way to data-collection terminals that can also scan the bar code. Other information about the transaction is also collected, such as the time and place of the transaction, other items purchased at the same time, sometimes the buyer's zip code and phone number, and the method of payment. That information is then electronically posted to a central computer at the end of the day or, in more advanced applications, instantly upon pressing the Enter key. The central computer may be in the same building or on the other side of the country, depending on the systems in place. Each transaction adds new value to the central database. Each use of the database, in turn, adds more information and more value for the organization. If one uses a credit or debit card to make a purchase, that information may be stored and a customer's lifestyle described by the purchases he or she makes. This "killer" application generated a distinct advantage for enterprises that had a deep understanding of their product or services and the market for them. "Deep understanding" of both product and market is a value-added element brought about by innovative applications of IT in its digital form.

Business, industry, and the military have become very adept at collecting, storing, and using data in ways unimagined in the days before the PC and the data network. The lesson for K–12 education is that the process has taken almost three decades, and it has been driven by competitive forces that are significantly absent in education. A short history of IT since 1960 is represented in table 2.1.

Table 2.1. Four Decades of Information Technology History

Decade	History of Information Technology
1960s	• Data processing comes of age around mainframe computers.
	• Early computer applications automated large-scale clerical operations such as inventory, personnel records, receipts, and disbursements.
	• Early applications were expensive to develop, and few systems of the time, if any, could communicate with others. Networks were nonexistent or very small and localized.
	• Data processing evolved into a "back room" culture with little or no involvement of management in day-to-day operations or systems development.
	• Data processing culture controlled how information technology (IT) was applied and who would use the resources and when.
	• Systems often ran over budget, failed to meet expectations, and were frequently abandoned before they were fully implemented.
	• The promise of empowerment was there, but lack of organizational knowledge about IT combined with traditional business practices conspired to block its emergence in the 1960s.
1970s	• The concept of management information systems (MISs) arrived in the middle of the decade.
	• Structured systems to generate standard reports were developed to address management's growing need for information.
	• The systems of the 1970s were also costly, and they, too, operated without management involvement in their planning and design. The back room culture maintained its control on IT.
	• Computers of the period had not developed the power to support enterprise-wide systems.
	• The recently experienced Y2K problem vividly illustrates the limitations that the 1970s technology imposed on systems.
	• Management had yet to learn that data by themselves do not equate to information, and knowledge and understanding were even further away.
	• Once data were converted to a useful form and delivered to those who needed it, they had lost much of their usefulness.
	• The notion of time sensitivity of data or shelf life of data was born.

Table 2.1. Four Decades of Information Technology History *(continued)*

Decade	*History of Information Technology*
	• The microcomputer arrived at the end of the decade, but few within traditional IT departments took notice.
1980s	• Personal computers arrived in the late 1970s and came of age in the early 1980s.
	• Skunk works and entrepreneurs taught organizations the value of shifting focus from MIS departments to looking outward to find ways to beat the competition through innovative uses of in-depth information.
	• By the late 1980s the concept of "just in time" for inventory, process changes, and so on became accepted.
	• Computers and then networks proliferated, but they remained largely proprietary with no commitment from vendors for cross-platform compatibility.
	• Vendors designed and developed hardware and software with an eye to being a "one-stop shop" for all IT needs.
1990s	• Experience with computers and networks proliferated vertically and horizontally throughout organizations.
	• The back room culture was out, and a revolution in business integration and reengineering was launched.
	• The IT industry responded by beginning to set standards for systems integration and data exchange.
	• The process of digital fusion started to bring computing and communicating together.
	• The Internet was adopted faster than any other communications medium in history.
	• The Internet itself became a force for setting standards for systems integration and data exchange.

As we enter the twenty-first century, organizations have learned to apply new IT technologies to a degree that has redefined the nature of power in the economy and in the nation-state. The motto for the last quarter of the twentieth century and the first quarter of the twenty-first century may well be "Knowledge is value" or "Knowledge is power." By the late 1980s, futurists were already speaking of the new knowledge-value revolution. In his book *PowerShift: Knowledge, Wealth, and Violence at the Edge of the 21st Century*, Alvin Toffler in 1990 speaks of "the astounding degree to which both force and wealth themselves have come to depend on knowledge."[1]

SCALE IS EVERYTHING

One of the lessons learned from the information revolution is that "size counts." Information technologies achieve their greatest significance when they can be applied across the big sky of megacorporations or government agencies. Data networks have connected corporate and government customers with their suppliers and manufacturers. In a web of synchronous and asynchronous communications possibilities, organizations have learned to do business at Internet speed. "Consolidate, merge, leverage" became battle cries as well as strategies for survival in an economy and political struggle that was and is global in scope. Profit is the driving force. The global IT industry has been predicted to reach $2 trillion by the year 2008. That does not count for the vast markets in other fields that have been consolidated around huge, global corporations. India, alone, had a $50 billion annual export of IT software and IT services (including IT-enabled services) by 1998.

SOME LESSONS LEARNED

- Integration of systems and processes adds value to organizational data.
- The stand-alone microcomputer has had a limited impact on "business as usual."
- Customization of applications produces the greatest benefit, but it is costly.
- IT resources must become pervasive in the organization along with the skills to use them appropriately before the full benefits of IT can be realized.
- Once IT applications begin to be used with effect, the organization will experience the absorption of more functions from old technologies into the new.
- Empowered with IT resources, end users can be keys to transformation.
- *Insight* and *understanding* are synonyms for knowledge gained through the mining of vast reservoirs of raw data, which has become the center of power and wealth in the modern world.
- Success comes from finding the right IT fit for an organization.
- In the beginning, experts tried to make one model fit everyone. They missed the power that derived from innovation, being first, and thinking and working outside of the box.

The way that traditional data-processing practitioners viewed and used IT became an issue of control that had to be overcome before IT could transform organizations. In K–12 and higher education today, few superintendents or principals have deep enough knowledge of basic IT tools and procedures to transition away from the DP back room. In the absence of competition for market share, educators have not had to be more productive or leverage their time or resources.

RIGHT SIZING AND REENGINEERING THE ORGANIZATION

The structural reorganization or reengineering that has reshaped business and industry around the globe has not touched the K–12 education industry to date. Consequently, most IT applications continue to be centralized and offer limited options to administrators. Although a few institutions and organizations are experimenting with integrated databases and site-based data processing, a large-scale movement does not seem likely within the K–12 education profession over the next five years.

Within higher education, however, the practice of traditional distance learning and asynchronous learning is beginning to impact the bottom line as colleges and universities find that it is both cheaper and more preferable for students to have at least part of their course offerings in nontraditional settings that are IT enabled. This usually means Web-based courses. We will discuss e-learning, distributed learning environments, and related issues later in this book.

THE FUTURE OF IT

The factors that have enabled IT to become fundamental to twenty-first-century society will continue to influence its development through 2020. As we have previously noted, the stand-alone microcomputer had a limited impact on business and government practices. However, once the microcomputer was integrated with other technologies, such as the data network, scanning or sensing devices, and communication protocols, everything began to change rapidly. Integration of hardware, software, and communication components has fueled the steady advance of IT. The industry will continue its advance toward full systems integration (around standards) as new technologies are brought on line and as existing technologies become more powerful, faster, and easier to use. Speech recognition for computer input along with advances in display technologies will significantly fuel IT use between 2001 and 2010. The near-term prospect for IT is for the present patterns of adoption and development to continue at accelerating rates. As pointed out in chapter 1, the laws of physics will support continued refinement of existing technologies up to about 2020 before theoretical limits are reached.

Improvements in transmission speeds will dramatically extend the use of IT into realms now served by traditional, analog video. Broadband, digital technologies are being widely deployed in 2001 and by 2010 will be universally available and used. Broadband infrastructures not only will change the speed and quality of information transmitted via global networks, they will launch new ventures and reduce reliance on existing resources and traditional practices. The pattern of absorption of more functions away from traditional resources and practices will continue, and the speed of absorption by new digital tools will increase.

For example, while video conferencing via Web-based systems is common today, the quality of the imagery leaves much to be desired. Anyone who has compared switched digital networks with video conferencing can appreciate the difference. While current video transmission is compressed and limited in resolution and image size, broadband, switched, digital video networks allow multiple sites to interact simultaneously with image quality equal to broadcast television. Bell Atlantic (now Verizon) has helped build these systems in Virginia and Maryland to support distributed learning. Similar applications are now used extensively for military training, especially in the U.S. Navy, in which personnel are frequently at sea and cannot attend traditional classes. The success of these and similar distributed learning environments is forming a foundation for broader implementation across the training and educational landscape.

CUSTOMIZATION

Another trend that will continue to extend the use and capabilities of IT, first in business and later in education, is the decreasing cost and difficulty of producing customized applications. Factors driving down these costs are advancements in development languages, new software tools, and the emergence of standards for data exchange. Standards for data communications fueled the "wiring" of society. Now standards for data exchange mean that an application developed by one vendor can share data and communicate with applications developed by others if they are developed to the same specifications.

Computer-assisted software engineering tools are also becoming more powerful and easier to use. Consequently, more firms are developing software than ever. The effort to scale up programming capabilities because of the Y2K issue has sent companies looking for new markets for their programming talent and will increase competition. Both of these factors mean that customized applications will soon become more widely used in K–12 schools. Although a program might not be written from "scratch" for a district or school, a systems integrator will be able to quickly pull together off-the-shelf components that are developed around data exchange and data format standards and integrate them with a minimum need for original programming code. The net impact of this kind of software will mean that schools can implement IT initiatives without completely revamping their practices just to accommodate a computer application. Given the relative vacuum of effective IT applications at the moment, K–12 education is likely to become a major market for IT applications between 2001 and 2010.

PERVASIVENESS

The increasing power of IT components and the growing affordability of customizable software will combine to make the spread of IT into society even more pervasive. As noted previously, "scale is everything." The more pervasive the development becomes, the greater the return on initial investments in IT development companies will realize. Increased profits will fuel more IT development as the cycle continues: technology feeding on the product of its own successes.

NOTE

1. Alvin Toffler, *PowerShift: Knowledge, Wealth, and Violence at the Edge of the 21st Century* (New York: Bantam Books, 1990), 17.

3

Educational Perspectives and Uses: Then and Now

THE 1980s

Generally, the early adoption and use of the microcomputer were similar to the adoption and use of other technologies when they were first introduced. One of the first uses of the motion picture camera, for example, placed it in a fixed position and aimed it at the theater stage to record the action as a member of the audience would experience it. It took time for the motion picture camera to come into its own. Risk takers moved the camera out of the theater and made it mobile. The field of cinematography was born. Shakespeare's line that "all the world's a stage" took on new meaning, and theater would never be the same.

The microcomputer was already showing up in K–12 schools by the late 1970s. The Commodore Pet, TRS-80 Model 1, and the Apple computer were among the first. The early interest was to make sure that children became familiar with computers and with what they could do. It did not take long, however, for someone to discover their "instructional potential." As with the motion picture camera, whose first use replicated an obvious, existing application, the idea that the computer would make an effective "teacher" or teaching machine reflected the same mind-set: "use new technology to accomplish old tasks."

Early treatises on computing in schools extol the virtues of computers as "patient tutors." "They never tire of prompting the student" was a familiar sales refrain. What that statement ignored was the fact that the student did tire rather quickly, even though the computer could keep beeping and clanging its "immediate feedback" to student "input" all day long. Working with the U.S. Office of Personnel Management in the early

1980s developing computer-based training (CBT) for government employees, I, Stallard, discovered that adults began to tire after an average of
about fourteen minutes of uninterrupted interaction with CBT (also called
computer-assisted instruction, or CAI). Longer periods of uninterrupted
CBT/CAI activity produced diminishing returns with these adults.

The attention spans of children and adolescents are comparable to those
of adults. When the way in which computers have been deployed in
schools (predominantly in computer labs) is combined with the way that
schools schedule time and the movement of students, teachers are effectively inhibited from using the resources within the fifteen- to twenty-
minute window that the attention span problem suggests. Once a computer
lab is scheduled and the class is moved into position, teacher and students
are likely to stay the full period. Indeed, the physical structure of schools
that organizes students into classroom groups of twenty to thirty-five inhibits approaches to instruction that would allow learners to move easily
from one activity to another. Such constraints effectively inhibit creative
uses of IT. Elementary-level classrooms have been more successful in using
IT because the classes are smaller, the day is less likely to be broken into
short, discrete periods, and the deployment of hardware has placed multiple computers into classrooms more often than in middle and high schools.

Hungry to break into and establish footholds in the education marketplace, the computer and software industries did a good job of extolling
the virtues of CAI. By the mid-1980s the belief was widespread that computers in schools were good things to have. Software vendors promoted
the view that plugging a student in to computer-based teaching programs
for extended periods would effectively raise test scores. Research during
the 1980s began to question the appropriateness of CAI as the primary use
for computers in K–12 education. However, the groundswell for placing
computers into schools was strong in the 1980s, and few took notice of the
controversy. Comprehensive "packages" or systems of instruction began
to be offered. Some of these covered an entire course of study. Dubbed the
integrated learning system, or ILS, these software packages delivered
"frames" of instruction with frequent quizzes to check for understanding.
Individuals and groups of students were tracked in terms of their
progress through the subject matter. The management piece of the ILS
was attractive to many teachers and administrators, and an industry arose
around integrated learning systems. Notice how schools' use of IT in the
early stages of adoption reflects the same mind-set that using the camera
to film a stage play did for early cinematographers. In both instances, a
new tool was used to replicate traditional practices. In the case of schools,
the computer became a teacher or deliverer of subject matter content.

With the arrival of the ILS and a growing library of simpler, individual
software packages, the Commodore Pet, the TRS-80, the Apple, and even-

tually the IBM PC and a family of clones exploded into classrooms. The Apple computer came to dominate the K–12 market during the 1980s and through the mid-1990s, but by the end of the century it had lost much of its lead to the "Wintel" platform (an acronym for Windows and Intel). All through the period, the driving force behind computer integration into K–12 education was the belief that the technology was a powerful teaching tool. As an instructional device, the computer replaced the teacher as deliverer of subject matter content. Whereas the business and government sectors found new uses for information technologies beyond computer-based training and created entirely new processes and new enterprises, educators stuck with their original application through much of the decade of the 1980s. In some respects, the K–12 profession is still focused on the teaching capabilities of computers to the exclusion of other possibilities, though new applications and processes are beginning to appear.

THE COMPUTER LAB MODEL OF COMPUTER INTEGRATION

It was common practice in K–12 schools in the 1980s to set up labs of twenty-five or thirty computers for entire classes of students to use at the same time. This seemed logical at the time given the way that space and time are structured in schools.

Teachers brought classes to the labs for computer-based instruction using whatever software the district had accumulated. Even then, these resources were likely to be used only if the teacher knew how to use and support the hardware and software or had a laboratory aide to handle the "techie" part of the lesson. Teacher training in computer use and integration did not happen on a significant scale until well into the 1990s. The lab model was attractive because computing resources were concentrated into one location. This simplified management and maintenance. Principals were often heard to complain that they had run out of space for new labs: "Every classroom has a teacher! Where am I supposed to put another computer lab?"

Such a view clearly indicates the mind-set that IT is something outside the regular school curriculum and supplemental to traditional instructional practices, something added on, and something for occasional attention and use. For many school leaders, the idea still has not occurred that IT belongs in every classroom. Likewise, K–12 educators have yet to realize that the lab approach may not be the most effective way to use IT in schools. Not only is it difficult to find space for something that is added on, it is more difficult to find time to incorporate anything new into an already full schedule of classes. IT in K–12 education still awaits acceptance as something that is routine, regular, and necessary for everyone. If the critics are right, most educators even today do not believe that IT will ultimately transform K–12 education, and it is the absence of that belief that keeps educators and vendors focused on the instructional use of computers and blind to other possibilities.

There are other factors that support the continuance of the computer lab model in schools. By having IT resources concentrated into a few locations, an instructional aide can be used to assist teachers with the hardware and software. If resources are distributed, their use will be more spontaneous rather than scheduled, as is lab use. Consequently, support for unskilled teachers will be more problematic. Also, providing technical aides for computer labs inhibits the natural pressures for every teacher to become a master of IT tools and resources. Labs lighten the teachers' load. It is no wonder that schools continue to support the lab model. It is an effective way to keep the technology at bay.

TEACHER TRAINING

When the computer first arrived at school, few teachers had prior experience with it. A few quickly developed a personal interest in learning about them, but the need to train teachers for computer utilization was largely neglected until the late 1990s. Schools, colleges, and departments of education (SCDEs) lacked both resources and interest in computer use in schools to offer meaningful pre-service training. Many SCDEs are only now beginning to think seriously about the need for IT training for teachers. They will have a difficult task ahead of them as they attempt to build faculty competence and infrastructures to support pre-service training that uses IT and teaches teachers how to use it in their professional careers. Similarly, the necessity for IT competence for school administrators and school support staff has not been realized by graduate schools, and that, too, keeps K–12 schools from seeing what has become obvious to leaders in other professions.

Government was slow to respond to the need for teacher training in IT. It was not until 1995, in a report to Congress entitled *Teachers and Technology: Making the Connection,* that the U.S. Office of Technology Assessment made it clear that schools, colleges, and departments of education were not meeting the challenge for pre-service training of teachers in the use of IT: "Despite the importance of technology in teacher education, it is not central to the teacher preparation experience in most colleges of education in the United States today. Most new teachers graduate from teacher preparation institutions with limited knowledge of the ways technology can be used in their professional practice."[1]

At the turn of the century, there was still no clear indication that SCDEs had taken up the challenge. A private group called the CEO Forum on Education and Technology was formed in 1996 as a four-year partnership between business and education leaders who were committed to facilitating the use of IT in U.S. schools. The forum has released a set of strategic documents for K–12 education. The first, *The School Technology Readiness Report: From Pillars to Progress* (October 1997), provides schools with a self-assessment tool to gauge their progress toward technology integration. The *CEO Forum StaR Chart*, as it has come to be called, has come out of that report and set benchmarks for infrastructure development, training, and application of IT by K–12 schools. The *StaR Chart* defines four levels of IT utilization for K–12 schools. The highest level, Target Tech, represented only about 6 percent of U.S. schools in 1998. Another CEO Forum report released in January 2000, *Teacher Preparation StaR Chart: A Self-Assessment Tool for Colleges of Education*, provides teacher education programs with benchmarks to use to measure their readiness to prepare teachers to integrate technology into their professional careers by using the technology in the undergraduate teacher-preparation program. The different reports of the CEO Forum and the *StaR Chart* can be found on the Internet at http://www.ceoforum.org.

In the absence of adequate skills to use IT effectively, K–12 institutions continue to rely on the lab model with lab aides providing assistance to teachers (or in many cases running the class for the teacher). The dedicated lab-plus-aide approach, while serving an immediate need to provide some level of IT experience for students, has actually had a negative impact on technology utilization in the long term. So long as aides are there to lean on, teachers can avoid developing the skills to use IT themselves. A combination of expectations for teachers and administrators to be competent users of IT and the provision of support by comprehensive programs of training and assessment is necessary to facilitate the integration of IT in K–12 education.

The lab or whole class approach to the use of computers in schools has mirrored what happened early in other organizations as traditional routines were automated or supplemented with IT tools. Cash registers became point-of-sale terminals. Credit cards were encoded with user identification and account information, and the ATM began replacing bank tellers. Computerized numerically controlled machines were introduced to the assembly line, and suddenly it seemed as if machines would replace humans in the production of most goods and services. Some commentators outside education have even dared to suggest that one day computers might also replace teachers. After all, they never get tired, never call in sick, and do not go on strike for higher wages or better working conditions.

Across society, the use of IT started by first adopting the technology to accomplish traditional tasks. During the 1980s, K–12 education was developing a familiarity with IT tools, a process that was necessary before new applications for IT could be invented. Institutions other than K–12 education found, adopted, and incorporated IT tools into their core business practices, and, because of them, they have reengineered and restructured their organizations in ways not possible before the PC. The workplace of the 2000s is very different from that of the 1970s. While we believe that by 2021 similar levels of transformation will have occurred in K–12 education, we do not assume that the agents of such change will come from within the education profession.

THE 1990s

The desktop computer by itself did not ignite the levels of change in the world that the decade of the 1990s witnessed. It took the development of another, related technology before IT could begin to change the very nature of human affairs. It was not faster CPU speeds or more processing power that brought the next quantum leap of IT applications to the private sector. The process by which computers communicate with one another and with other devices became standardized and became simpler to manage in the 1990s. It is the arrival of the computer network combined with open standards for electronic communications that has fueled one of the greatest gains in productivity in our history.

If the decade of the 1980s is classified as the decade of the microcomputer, then the decade of the 1990s clearly has to be the decade of the network. The push to put desktop computers in schools paled in comparison with the effort to wire the schools for "access." Of course, it took a "killer" application to create the networking frenzy that K–12 education experienced during the 1990s. That application was the Internet. Before the Internet was widely recognized as an educational resource, business and industry had discovered the power of electronic communications and applied that power to transform the nature of business and business relationships. The concept of "leveraging" resources took on new meaning in networked environments.

A resource is leveraged when it is used to the maximum extent. Leveraging expensive computer peripherals was one of the first factors that led to the development of local area networks. Business, industry, and then governments recognized the savings that such connectivity offered. Standard protocols that allow computers and peripherals to communicate with one another over copper wires were developed even before the arrival of the microcomputer. In the early days of the industry, vendors of computer hardware envisioned becoming a "one-stop shop" for all of a client's electronic data-processing needs, and each developed its own proprietary systems for data connections and communications. IBM, for example, promoted its Token Ring technology and quickly dominated the market for data communications. If one bought IBM equipment, it had to be connected to peripherals that were made by IBM using IBM connectivity solutions and IBM software. As it developed, the IT industry began to recognize the need for a more open market and developed and adopted open systems and open standards for data communications. A set of protocols for data communications emerged in the 1980s and is referred to as the OSI model—or open systems interconnection. OSI gradually established itself, and proprietary systems began to fall by the wayside.

Ethernet, a protocol for sending packets of data over wires or fibers, eventually became an industry standard and widely replaced IBM's Token Ring and others. All of this is significant because the movement toward open systems and standards drove down the prices of network components to a point at which by the early 1990s pioneering schools and districts could afford to begin installing local and even wide area networks. Educators began to discover, as others already had, that networks can leverage more than hardware.

Networks link people electronically, and, being linked, human resources can also be leveraged. Electronic connections enable new forms of communications. Asynchronous communications (those not concurrent in time) via electronic mail have quickly outpaced synchronous communications (sending and receiving a message concurrent in time) as in traditional telephone systems. Consider the number of e-mail messages you receive on an average day versus the number of telephone calls you receive. Asynchronous communications leverage employee time. Less time is spent redialing because of busy signals, and less time is spent leaving messages playing the "telephone tag" game. Networks quickly propagated bulletin board systems where groups could share communications (sometimes called threaded discussion groups), another asynchronous mode of communication. On-line communities or electronic villages developed and pressed the networking and telecommunications industry with the demand for low-cost, reliable connectivity that continues unabated today.

Asynchronous communications has had an impact on the way in which educators view information technology. It took nothing less than the Internet to draw attention away from strictly instructional programs or direct teaching via the computer.

EDUCATIONAL USE OF TECHNOLOGY CHANGES DIRECTION

By the mid-1990s, collections of information on bulletin boards and later on the Internet were quickly seen as useful teaching and learning resources and caused some educators to look beyond the computer as a teacher to something much more significant, that is, a new learning/teaching resource. Once schools had access to human experts on the Web who were willing to collaborate with students and teachers, K–12 education had another impetus to connect schools. Early work at San Francisco's Exploratorium has served as a prototype for other museums and agencies to become more directly involved in K–12 education. Students and teachers submitted questions or problems to scientists at the Exploratorium who would in turn respond, asynchronously, through e-mail or bulletin board posts. The Exploratorium institutionalized support for K–12 education as part of its mission. The venue for K–12 education seemed poised to shift from classrooms to the world at large. Visit the Exploratorium website at http://www.exploratorium.edu/.

If not the predominate influence, certainly, the Internet and its successors will be major factors shaping K–12 education between now and 2021. By 2001, higher education has firmly established distance or distributed learning as a strong component of its programs. The military and the government have likewise employed distance learning to reduce costs, improve efficiency, and extend the reach of their training and development programs. Business and industry are also highly dependent on the lifelong learning of employees, and much of that learning is based on Internet resources and activities. Every indication is that other public agencies and the private sector will come to rely almost exclusively on electronic communications for training and development in the future. What about K–12 education? How far will it go with the concept of virtual schools and virtual learning communities?

There are numerous experiments in 2001 with distributed learning via the Internet. Satellite-based distance learning systems have also carved a small niche in K–12 education. States such as Maryland and Virginia, among others, have extensive switched digital video networks in place to support distance learning. These use broadcast-quality video and very expensive private broadband networks to support learning that is synchronous in nature (teachers and students are together at the same time but at different places, each viewing and speaking to the others). Virtual schools in Canada, Florida, and elsewhere are beginning to test the viability of the concept of "classrooms without walls." Chapter 6 will take an in-depth look at the distributed learning movement and its role to 2021. However, before looking too far into the future, there are other elements of the K–12 environment that have to be considered before the future can be placed into perspective.

The experience of others who have been more impacted by IT suggests that the next two decades will bring very different uses of IT to schools. Just as new uses were invented for business, government, and the military, new uses will emerge in K–12 education. The political, economic, and demographic pressure for schools to change is growing and will eventually reach a point at which it can no longer be ignored. New uses will not come as easily as some may think. They will not come without some pain on the part of educators who will have to invent new roles for themselves in the process. Education poses some unique challenges to the IT industry that must be overcome for transformation to occur.

NOTE

1. U.S. Office of Technology Assessment, *Teachers and Technology: Making the Connection*, GPO stock #052-003-01409-2, Government Printing Office (April 1995), 2. Available at http://www.ota.nap.edu/pdf/1995idx.html.

4

Challenges to the IT Industry Posed by Public Education

Public K–12 education often is not what it seems. The lay observer may walk into schools anywhere in the United States and, on first glance, see what appear to be essentially the same things happening. The texts will be the same, the classrooms will look much the same, and teachers and school staff may even dress alike. Appearance can be deceiving, however. Each school district and each school is different in many ways. Also, the differences among them are of a different kind than, say, differences between a J. C. Penney department store in Minneapolis and one in Dallas. Schools reflect the communities they serve almost as a mirror reflects the image of the person gazing into it. Businesses, government, and military institutions reflect their institutional cultures first and then attempt to fit in with the local market or into the larger context in which they find themselves. Their goals, strategies, and business practices remain essentially the same from place to place. This is not so with schools. Not only do schools take on the flavor of their communities, they are further defined by the leadership within the district and within the building. The tastes, values, and priorities of key individuals influence both process and content in public schools. These differences create unique market conditions and pose unique problems for the adoption and use of IT.

LOCAL CONTROL

One of the major challenges posed to the adoption and use of IT by schools is tied to the issue of local control of public education. Hardware and software vendors alike have to consider local preferences and practices when planning what they will bring to market and on what schedule. Day-to-day operational requirements have evolved differently among schools and districts, thereby limiting the size of the market for any one IT resource. Further, some degree of customization is required for virtually any management or analysis software. Shrink-wrapped solutions do not fit a broad spectrum of the K–12 education market. At the same time, differences in performance standards and curriculum requirements among the states compound the difficulty of developing digital content for a fractured market. Even something as basic as subject area content in British literature differs from district to district and reflects local tastes and values. Each region, and in some cases each district within a region, must be viewed as a different market. These smaller markets do not attract large-scale investment or promote complex software development as larger markets do. Consequently, K–12 institutions tend to have less sophisticated tools with which to work.

MULTIPLE CPU PLATFORMS

As discussed in chapter 3, the K–12 school market is further fractured by the presence of different computing platforms. Something developed for the Wintel platform has to also be developed for the Macintosh or Linux platform if the vendor is going to reach that particular market segment. Fractured markets compound development processes and increase production costs while simultaneously limiting returns on investments made for any segment of the market; in other words, as with software, the education market for a particular CPU is fractured. This obstacle may no longer be a factor once the World Wide Web becomes the primary venue for both digital curriculum content and educational program applications. Applications and digital content delivered over the Web are platform independent. Also, as software becomes more of a service as opposed to a shrink-wrapped product that the end user owns, installs, and maintains, platform will become less of an obstacle. The software industry seems poised to transform itself into a service industry as the Internet becomes universally accessible to schools and as the bandwidth available to the classroom increases. In its report entitled *Trends Shaping the Digital Economy*,[1] the Software and Information Industry Association (SIIA) predicts that by 2002 the software industry will deliver significantly more of its product as a service rather than as a product in the traditional sense. As in the past, the private sector has set the pace, and by 2002 about 70 percent of new e-business software will be provided in such a fashion, according to the report. The report was issued in July 2000 and is available from the SIIA through its website at http://www.trendsreport.net.

It has been suggested that one productive role for the federal government in improving K–12 education is to finance software development when the private sector will not assume the risk. We must point out, however, that there is no guarantee that the federal government has the insight to know what to develop or the ability to manage such a process even if it were willing to assume the financial burden. In spite of years of research into computer-enabled learning, the federal government still wants to spend time and money doing research on "what works and what does not." By "what works" the government means which teaching applications produce the highest test scores and little else. For the foreseeable future, the fractured nature of the K–12 educational software market will likely remain with consolidation of some markets around the Internet and standard protocols. New developments that do occur will occur within this context. In 2001, the Internet has become the focus of much of commerce and education. Undoubtedly something bigger and better lies beyond the Internet, but what it is still is not apparent from our vantage point in 2001.

READINESS TO USE IT

Districts and schools vary in their readiness to utilize IT in general and networked resources in particular. While many schools and classrooms have been equipped with computers and printers, and most have now been wired, low levels of maintenance and support combined with inadequately trained and motivated teachers inhibit the use of IT. One of the key issues around maintenance and support of school technology has asked the question, "To what degree should end users be expected to be self-sufficient in troubleshooting problems with software and hardware?" Even in larger secondary schools that have one or more full-time technical support persons, complex networks and the presence of hundreds or thousands of workstations prove overwhelming, and teaching staffs are still required to be self-sufficient with IT in several ways. Learning to maintain electronic resources competes with learning to integrate them into the curriculum and also competes with the other functions that school personnel have to support each day. As any classroom teacher will tell you, the day is not getting any longer. Everything still has to be fit within the same time period.

The readiness or condition of the school building itself frequently presents significant obstacles to appropriate IT use. Inadequate electrical service can be overcome by adequate funding, but structural restraints, such as fixed classroom sizes, and the physical layout of the building often inhibit what are potentially the most productive uses of

IT resources. Classrooms, for example, are designed to accommodate thirty or more students and are ill-suited for work by small groups or for collaborative projects. The shape and size of traditional classrooms tend to dictate the "Sage on the Stage" approach to instruction. While good lectures remain an important instructional technique, other approaches can be better in given situations. The physical space of a school should accommodate all modes of instruction.

Surprisingly, new school construction has not changed to meet the challenges of IT as a teaching and learning resource. Architects and construction and maintenance departments of school divisions alike seem unable to see beyond the "boxes-in-a-box" architecture of traditional school design. Designing schools with flexible spaces that can accommodate differently sized groups and different kinds of learning and teaching activities remains an exception rather than the rule.

For the foreseeable future, there is no apparent solution on the horizon to the problem of inadequate school spaces for technology utilization. Some critics of K–12 education argue that the school as a physical place will fade away, replaced by a model of distributed learning that involves the entire community. We do not see this as a likely scenario. Schools that are built over the next twenty years will look very much like those built in the last two decades of the twentieth century. Changes, if they come at all, will come late in that period. This is not to say that communities will continue to rely as heavily on schoolhouses as places where children learn. We do feel that schoolhouses will persist in the landscape well beyond our time frame of 2001–21. What goes on inside will change somewhat, but schoolhouses and schoolteachers are not endangered species at this time. Schoolhouses and the people who staff them perform a broad range of social services, and they will very probably assume more noninstructional duties with each passing year. At the same time, we expect to see movement toward using new service providers for the design and delivery of instruction. We expect the rate of change in this respect to be quite slow in the near term.

INTELLECTUAL INCEST

The persistence of traditional school architecture may be the best example of the lack of awareness and understanding educators have of how IT has impacted the rest of society and how society is changing. Educators have long been known for their "intellectual incest" or tendency to look only within their discipline for ideas and direction. A brief excursion into the recent history of military and business practices would offer a new perspective on what is possible within the networked, electronically empowered world we have created. Schools, colleges, and departments of education offer little relief in this respect. This is true for teacher training programs and for graduate studies in school management and administration. Educators write for educators, and educators read primarily within their professional literature. Cross-fertilization from other fields is not common. Intellectual incest presents one of the strongest obstacles to change of any kind within K–12 education. To a significant degree, the failure of educators at all levels to grasp the nature of information technologies and the degree to which they are bringing structural changes to society is tied to their narrow specialization. The exposure they are getting to the field of IT is limited to simple suggestions about how to integrate it with everything else going on in the curriculum and has little to do with understanding the phenomenon of the digital revolution.

IT ORGANIZATION

How the function of IT is administratively organized within school districts creates differences in perception about its value and which IT resources should be utilized by schools. When the desktop computer first arrived, the reaction by most governing boards and superintendents was to hand over control to those in their organizations who had the longest history with computing and networking. Consequently, IT quickly became the domain of the operations side of the district's management and was administratively located under assistant superintendents for operations or support services. Business and industry, on the other hand, moved away from the culture of the "back room" data-processing shop and by the mid-1980s had learned to organize IT around the business side of their enterprises. The result ended back office or data processing (DP) control of data, its flow, and how IT resources were used in the organization. Instead, these were driven by the business side of the enterprise, the point-of-sale aspect.

The business side of K–12 education is the classroom, the equivalent to the point-of-sale terminal or the ATM that we find in retail and banking. If K–12 institutions had organized IT around the classroom or, better yet, around the learning process of individual students, platforms and infrastructures would have evolved differently. K–12 school management information system (MIS) departments have traditionally designed IT resources for ease of use, lowest cost of installation, and how thoroughly the resource can be centrally controlled. K–12 MIS departments are highly motivated to improve the efficiency of their operations, frequently at the expense of what is the preferred solution for the learning process. Given the typical background of those on the operations side of school district management, it is not difficult to understand why they take that approach. They have no understanding for the learning side and simply do not understand the business they are in. Even those in charge of what goes on in classrooms have difficulty recognizing the nature of their business. When educators are asked what business they are in, they inevitably answer "instruction" when the real product of schooling should be learning.

Too often, the MIS or DP function drives the nature of the technologies going into classrooms, libraries, and laboratories. Logistics and support for IT in educational settings present a tremendous task, and placing IT on the instructional side of the house can complicate everything else MIS is asked to do, and that is another reason why people resist such a move.

Rather than blame the operations side of school administration for its failure to understand the instructional or business side, it is probably more appropriate to ask why the instructional side has not risen to the challenge to understand IT and take control of such important resources. Beyond the fact that few instructional leaders have been prepared in their graduate studies or in their prior work careers to do so, there are political factors that often influence how IT is organized and used within public school districts.

Boards of education at the state and local level frequently assume control of the decision-making process. In certain states, for example, the state department of education has adopted standards for the IT resources that school districts can purchase. In the arena of setting standards for hardware and software for entire states, the IT industry has tremendous motivation to influence those decisions in any way possible. Billions of dollars can be at stake over time. State education agencies are no less susceptible than are local school districts in terms of relying on traditional MIS groups within their organizations to define IT standards and practices. Again, the logic and rationale for these decisions are not likely to rest on what is best for the learning environment. Most likely, they will reflect the management biases brought to the table. Then, too, decisions are sometimes made in an effort to support local industries and businesses. A close look at early efforts in Britain to use only "made here" technology in their schools reveals the folly of such priorities.

Trends in society in general and changing expectations of state departments of education in particular are likely to crack the traditional MIS hold on IT resources in K–12 education in the coming years. Demands for assessment data around specific standards of learning that are coming from all levels of government coupled with a growing expectation from the public for more personalized services will eventually lead to IT management in K–12 schools that is organized around the classroom and the individual learner. The process, however, will take at least another decade to materialize. But already forward-thinking school districts are positioning themselves to meet these expectations.

PROCUREMENT PRACTICES

Technology changes rapidly. Training, installation, maintenance, and support for school-based IT resources are complex. K–12 schools' IT departments are usually understaffed to meet the need. Add to this mix frustratingly slow and complex procurement processes, common among public school districts, and it is not hard to understand why so many educators would rather not bother with IT. Bureaucratic procedures usually mean that orders for even basic supplies can take months to process. It is not uncommon to hear stories about an IT product that has gone out of production by the time bids or requests for proposals can be generated and processed. Business and industry, on the other hand, have learned to forge strategic alliances and relationships with vendors and suppliers to provide "just-in-time" resources. Public education, unlike its private counterpart, is admonished from talking with vendors or manufacturers in the fear that some impropriety or an appearance of one will cause scandal. Over time, the public sector will also have to learn to build alliances across a wide range of businesses and organizations in order to provide the level of services its public will demand. Change will come slowly, and we do not expect major movement on this issue for at least another ten years.

LOGISTICS

Once a resource is purchased and received, delay in delivery and installation often adds another layer of frustration for end users. One way around this problem is to purchase installation with the resource itself. Doing so increases total cost and reduces the number of resources a district can purchase with a limited budget. Even a medium-sized district is likely to purchase several hundred new computers and printers during a school year, and a larger district will purchase thousands. Warehouse space and work areas for the installation of software and hardware are hard to find or nonexistent in the typical school district.

Combined with the difficulty of procurement, logistical problems frustrate teachers and administrators alike to the point at which coming to depend on IT is a risky business. Student performance on test scores are the bottom line for educators, and anything that detracts from or consumes instructional time gets little attention. The short-term prospect for change in procurement and logistics is not good. That fact will impact how districts that have become dependent on IT in their day-to-day operations will acquire the services of IT as well as hardware and software products. If it is too cumbersome a process to purchase, install, and maintain hardware and software resources within the district itself, school districts may begin to look in earnest for private groups to provide the same services. In 2000, for example, the school district of Detroit, Michigan, decided to outsource its entire IT operation. While other districts have outsourced one or more functions of IT, this may be the first case in which a district as large as Detroit has decided to outsource the entire operation. In the case of software, outsourcing may take the form of applications being offered from a central, private group of servers or via the Internet.

Unfortunately, at the moment, the IT industry does not know enough about the institution of K–12 education to be able to adequately serve it in this fashion. Pricing strategies, product offerings, and service contracts that are standard in the industry in 2001 do not meet the needs of K–12 institutions. As IBM and other large companies have learned over the past twenty years, it is not possible to lift traditional IT practices out of business, military, or government markets and apply them to education. The prospects for the emergence of a service sector within the IT industry that has a real capability to meet the needs of K–12 education are good. However, they are not likely to be realized until 2010 or beyond.

Some smaller districts have learned to form regional consortia to share services and are realizing significant savings due to volume. Also, consortia of districts are able to offer services together that single districts alone could not afford or support. In response to the need for collaborative efforts among districts, the U.S. Department of Education, through its Office of Educational Research and Improvement, issued a competitive request for proposals that resulted in funding six Regional Technology in Education Consortia under Title III of the Elementary and Secondary Education Act of 1965. Title III is also known as the Technology for Education Act of 1994. These consortia conduct regional activities that address professional development, technical assistance, and information resource dissemination designed to meet the needs in the region they serve and to foster regional cooperation and resource sharing. Then, there are locally initiated consortia such as South Bay Advanced Educational Technology (ADTECH) Consortium in Redondo Beach, California. The ADTECH Consortium brings together schools, businesses, and professionals in the community in an effort to unite and leverage resources and provide services to the diverse areas of the South Bay. The consortium is a partnership of thirteen school districts, 120 schools, more than 100,000 students, parents, universities and community colleges, government agencies, and industry parties. Participating business organizations represent over 10,000 South Bay employers. Such a diversified consortium will understand the value and importance of technology in today's and tomorrow's world and relieve the problem of intellectual incest among educators. The development educational technology consortia are a growing trend and will be a force for positive change in K–12 education. They will also help the private sector better understand and appreciate the diversities and complexities of K–12 education. At the moment it is the absence of collaboration or consortia that is another inhibitor of IT utilization.

MYTH OF THE VAST EDUCATION MARKET

When one looks casually at the size of the education market, it seems to be so large that that private enterprise has little to lose by competing for a share of it. Expenditures for public K–12 and higher education exceeded $650 billion in 1998 and are projected to reach $1 trillion by 2004 according to the U.S. Department of Education. Education is a large market and a growing one, at least for the short term. The U.S. Bureau of the Census estimates that the number of children aged five to seventeen grew from 45.1 million in 1988 to 51.1 million in 1998. The bureau also projects this to increase slightly to 52.8 million by the end of 2008. Growing numbers of school-aged children translate directly into increasing public and private school enrollment levels at least for most of the decade between 2001 and 2010. The National Center for Education Statistics projects that the total enrollment in public and private elementary and secondary schools will grow to approximately 54.3 million by 2008.

To better understand expenditures on K–12 education, consider the following data taken from a U.S. Department of Education National Center for Education Statistics 1998 report entitled *Overview of Public Elementary and Secondary Schools and Private School Survey:*

Total Public Schools	82,631
Total Private Schools	27,402
Total Expenditures	$650 billion

When K–12 budgets are analyzed in detail, however, it becomes apparent that only a small percentage of this sum is potentially available to the private sector. Consider the analysis in figure 4.1, also provided by the U.S. Department of Education National Center for Education Statistics.

For a significant portion of the education dollar to be available to the IT industry, traditional practice will have to change. There is very little discretionary money available to public schools. Most funds are spent on teacher salaries and benefits. Unless other classroom management and instructional delivery methods are employed to change the ratio of

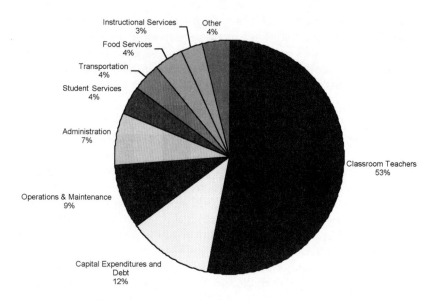

Figure 4.1. How Education Spends Its Money

labor to resources cost, this portion of school budgets will remain unavailable. Likewise, with the other areas of the K–12 education budget, traditional approaches to schooling requires all of these funds. For education, IT is an added cost. Perhaps some funds for textbooks or library reference materials are being diverted to IT, but the percentage is quite small. Clearly, for K–12 education to evolve as a market that attracts investment dollars and the creation of new tools and resources, traditional practice will have to change in ways that allow IT resources to supplant traditional practice instead of supplementing it in a very minor way. Of the approximately $6.8 billion spent each year in the United States on instructional materials, only about 10 percent is spent on digital content. One way to bring more IT resources into schools will be to divert funds spent on nondigital materials. For more information on the nature of public education budgets and some analysis of trends, see the U.S. Department of Education National Center for Education Statistics website at http://nces.ed.gov/ccd.

UNEVEN FUNDING FOR IT

For schools and districts to fully adopt and realize the benefits of IT in teaching, learning, and managing schools, adequate and reliable levels of funding must first be established. So long as IT is viewed as an add-on to the traditional process of running schools, it will be among the first thing to be cut when budgets become tight. The uneven pattern of funding for IT over the past twenty years has hindered its adoption in public education. State initiatives tend to be spotty. Different legislatures place different levels of importance on the presence of IT in schools, and funding has been unpredictable. Likewise, federal dollars, though relatively small, come and go. Even the e-Rate program has not lived up to its promises in terms of providing dependable funding from year to year. Strategic and long-range planning are hindered so long as districts have little feel for what their funding will be from one year to the next.

ATTITUDES AMONG EDUCATORS

It is standard practice in 2001 to argue that the great obstacle to IT utilization in K–12 education stems from the fact that teachers have not been trained to use it appropriately. Federal funds for educational technology usually come with the requirement that a significant percentage be used for training. We would not disagree that training is an essential component, but, at the same time, it is not uncommon to find cases in which training has been emphasized for several years and levels of utilization are still quite low. Something other than training is keeping teachers and administrators from using IT as they could and should. We discussed some of these factors when we outlined the problems with procurement, installation, and maintenance above. Beyond these things, which some like to use as handy excuses for their lack of use of IT resources, many educators really prefer not to bother with it.

Teaching, they say, is more of an art than a science. It is a transaction between a teacher and the class. Computers and other machines create "noise" in that communication process and detract from what the teacher is doing. Whether teaching is art or science is hardly the question. Schools are not in the business of instruction or curriculum development. The intended product of schooling is learning. Learning is the only product that counts. Learning or its absence constitutes the bottom line in education. Strangely, that fact seems lost on most K–12 schools. One will find departments of instruction and sometimes departments of curriculum but never a department of learning.

Teachers insisting on freedom to be "artistic" in the classroom present a major obstacle to the effective use of IT. Art happens or it does not. Real artistic talent is rare in any field, and many times what is intended as art is more craft. To assume that our society can produce one million or more teachers who can effectively practice teaching as an art is absurd, even if it were desirable. Creating environments to support the learning of human individuals should proceed on the basis of understanding. Understanding is derived from analysis, reasoning, and the manipulation of information about the learner and the nature of learning more than it is from understanding the discipline or subject one teaches. So long as teachers put themselves first in the processes of schooling with the emphasis on teaching their disciplines as art, learners will continue to fall short of realizing their real potential.

THE BUSINESS AS USUAL MENTALITY

So long as each teacher is expected to design, produce, and deliver each lesson each time it is taught, teachers will have inadequate time to learn to use IT or to apply it to their particular learning environments. It is a sad commentary that K–12 education expects one person to fit six or seven hours of classroom teaching and management into an eight-hour day and be fully prepared with individualized teaching styles, materials, and strategies to meet the needs of twenty-five children in elementary grades or more than 100 in the upper grades. In secondary schools in particular, teachers may have three or four different courses to prepare each day.

There is no humanly possible way that each lesson can be fully developed to meet the individual needs of each child in such a model. The teachers know this and argue for fewer classroom contact hours and fewer independent preparations. They argue for these along with smaller class sizes. Boards of education point out that they simply cannot afford an increase in school budgets by 30 to 50 percent to meet the labor requirements to provide these conditions, and they are right.

It is absurd to assume that one human being can bring to the K–12 school classroom what government, military, and industry bring to their training and personnel development programs. In the 1980s, while I, Stallard, was working on a project for the Office of Personnel Management of the federal government, it was a surprise to learn that, for government or military applications, about 1,000 man-hours of preparation would go into each hour of lesson product. The lesson product included content, materials, and very specific strategies for implementing the lesson. At the same time, those chosen to instruct were not the individuals who were contracted to develop the lessons themselves. Subject matter experts formed teams with instructional designers, graphic artists, multimedia and video programmers, human factor engineers, and psychologists to produce validated courses and assessments.

The "business as usual" mentality of K–12 schools precludes any movement toward something called differentiated staffing, whereby some do design work and produce courses while others implement them in the classroom. Instead, each teacher designs, develops, delivers, and assesses each lesson each time it is taught. Even within the same school, two teachers teaching the same senior English class will develop lessons independent from one another. Getting past the mind-set that each teacher does his or her thing with his or her subject and students has to be a top priority for K–12 education. IT will facilitate a shift toward centrally developed and validated lessons and assessments. IT will eventually assume more of the role of delivery of instruction. Both of these eventualities will be long in coming, however. Do not look for dramatic change in standard operational procedures in schools for at least another fifteen years.

As with lesson development, delivery, and assessment, so too is it a business as usual mentality when it comes to the use of data to inform the day-to-day operations of schools and classrooms. So long as schools do not have a systematic way to collect "business-side" data from the transactions they engage in routinely (planning, teaching, testing, managing), it is not reasonable to expect them to be able to provide highly individualized learning environments. It is equally unreasonable to expect anything like continuous improvement in learning when feedback about the success or failure of strategies and resources is so lacking. Centralizing lesson development around in-depth information about each learner who will experience the lesson is a radical departure from classrooms in which the teacher does everything. In large part this is an issue of control, and teachers do not want to relinquish it.

So, while it may be true that IT resources in K–12 education have not yet reached a point at which they are reliable, easy to use, and readily accessible, teachers often resist their use and prefer a business as usual approach to their classrooms. Teacher and administrator attitudes will have to change, followed by changes in how schools are operated, if K–12 education as we know it today ever fully embraces the use of IT. Paying lip service to the need to integrate IT will never be enough. Formal reformulation of the roles and duties of educators will be required for real change to occur in this area, and such change will come slowly. Unless educators suddenly face severe competition from another institution, they are unlikely to change at all. We expect to see little movement in this respect in the near-term future.

PUBLIC EDUCATION MONOPOLY

Attitudes toward IT and toward the real purpose and processes of schooling have to change dramatically in order for significant progress to occur in either general educational effectiveness or the appropriate uses of IT by schools. The prospect for change is not good for the near term. The competitive nature of business and of military operations forced change in those arenas. Public education, at the moment, has no real competition. That could change as state and federal governments continue to play with the idea of vouchers and charter schools. Even if both practices become common, there is no guarantee that new private schools or charter schools will approach the task of K–12 education with a different mind-set. It is likely to be the same individuals who run public schools today who will assume control of increased numbers of private schools or charter schools. For competition to be effective as a change agent, it will have to come from an entirely different place.

Venture capital for educational enterprises is limited at the moment in spite of the fact that public K–12 and higher education in the United States accounts for nearly 10 percent of the U.S. gross domestic product for the year. Only spending for health care products and services has exceeded this market. Trend analysis shows that education spending has nearly doubled over the past ten years, at a rate of approximately 7 percent per year. Based on such trends and the growing importance of education to the national well-being, it is not unreasonable to anticipate a $1 trillion industry by 2004. That figure will continue to increase as the Information Age gives way to the Age of Knowledge and lifelong learning becomes more urgent for more people. When private enterprise finally learns how to deal with a market that consists of more than 115,000 K–12 schools, housing 52 million learners, at a cost of approximately $6,500 per student per year, serious competition for what is now public K–12 education may finally arrive. This does not even take into account the impact of the need for lifelong learning for everyone. No one has a handle on the size of that market or can foresee how large it will become by 2021.

The fact remains that as revolutionary as technological advances have been over the past twenty years, and in spite of burgeoning workplace trends that are mandating lifelong learning, we still wait for an innovative entrepreneur to introduce a creative solution for how to support learning in ways that significantly challenge traditional practice. The Internet represents the strongest move forward to date, but how to leverage the Internet to provide the right mix of services and content has yet to be defined. Undoubtedly, more learning activity will become focused on the Internet each year, but the prospects for the current services and applications that are available on the Web to seriously challenge the dominant position of public schools are not good. As broadband reaches homes by 2005 and beyond, two-way interactive systems may begin to make a challenge. For that to significantly impact public education, we have to look to 2015 and beyond.

PRE-SERVICE TEACHER TRAINING

In a report to Congress in 1995 entitled *Teachers and Technology: Making the Connection*, the U.S. Office of Technology Assessment stated: "Despite the importance of technology in teacher education, it is not central to the teacher preparation experience in most colleges of education in the United States today. Most new teachers graduate from teacher preparation institutions with limited knowledge of the ways technology can be used in their professional practice."[2] Other reports since 1995 suggest that little has changed. The CEO Forum, in its 2000 publication entitled *Teacher Preparation StaR Chart: A Self-Assessment Tool for Colleges of Education,* states: "Today, less than half of the nation's teacher preparation institutions require students to design and deliver instruction using technology. Even fewer require technology use in the student teaching experience. Since less than half of the faculty in teacher preparation programs incorporate effective uses of technology in their courses, perhaps this is not surprising."[3]

While K–12 schools and districts have invested in hardware, software, and infrastructure, and while they have also assumed the burden of teacher training for technology education, institutions of higher education have not made similar investments. Getting the necessary IT resources and infrastructure in place will require time. It will also take time to get faculty prepared for the task. The prospect for teacher preparation programs to make a real difference in teacher readiness to use IT is not good for at least the next seven to ten years—and then only if a concerted effort is made to start the process immediately. Given that about 2.5 million new teachers will enter the workforce by 2010, consider the difficulty that school districts face promoting IT utilization to so many unprepared teachers.

It would help a great deal for the short term if new approaches to preservice teacher education could be implemented. Just as private enterprise has assumed a large share of the postgraduate education market in highly skilled fields, so may public school districts and consortia of districts assume bigger roles in the certification process of teachers. Public schools have more IT resources and have a longer history of teacher training in technology utilization in spite of the failure of their employees to embrace it fully. Selected districts that have demonstrated capabilities in terms of resources and infrastructures and have demonstrated strong IT applications perhaps should take on the challenge of pre-service teacher training just as hospitals have become teaching institutions for doctors and nurses.

As large numbers of veteran educators retire over the next few years, the need for new teachers casts the long shadow of potential shortages across all regions of the United States. State and local agencies have responded with alternatives to traditional, university-based teacher education. States such as California, New Jersey, and Arizona had alternative programs in place by the late 1980s. These were not designed around high-performing school districts, however, and candidates' skills and abilities in the use of IT were never a factor in their implementation. These and other alternatives have allowed institutions of higher education to protect their interests by requiring baccalaureate degrees as a condition of enrollment. In an article published in the *Journal of Teacher Education*,[4] the American Association of Colleges for Teacher Education states its position on alternative certification. Its position calls for higher certification standards to be managed by schools, colleges, and departments of education (SCDEs). At the very least, alternative certification programs should include a baccalaureate degree as a prerequisite; assessment of subject matter competency, personal characteristics, and communications skills; a curriculum that provides knowledge and skills essential to the beginning teacher; and a supervised internship. Given the resistance of SCDEs to the idea of nontraditional teacher certification programs that do not include them, change in this area is not likely by 2021. Teacher training in IT use will continue to fall to the districts themselves as in-service training. Some may develop consortia for the purpose, and others may outsource to private vendors or even to SCDEs, but the responsibility will remain with the districts.

ADMINISTRATOR TRAINING

Just as teacher training programs fall short of the mark in terms of preparing classroom professionals with skills and insights about how to use IT resources, so too do graduate programs in educational administration fail to provide the skills and insights that principals, directors, supervisors, and superintendents need in order to assume leadership duties in their districts. If site-based administrators do not know what good instructional practice looks like when it comes to IT integration and use, it is not reasonable to expect them to fulfill leadership roles in making IT central to the day-to-day business of their schools. Similarly, few school administrators have insights into how to make best use of "business-side" data and information to inform their routine management and instructional decisions. A typical urban high school may have as many as 2,000 students and 200 employees, offering a few hundred different courses of study. An enterprise of this size presents a large management task. If you are a businessperson reading this, imagine tackling that with 1970s approaches to IT, and you have a pretty accurate picture of school management practice today.

A principal or superintendent who knows technology and information management is a rare commodity and extremely valuable. As districts insist on these qualities for new hires, an opportunity for private organizations to train and certify administrators in IT management and instructional leadership for IT integration will present itself. As with teachers, it is unlikely that colleges of education will be able to meet this challenge in time. Already, one can find hints of what is to come on the Internet as professional groups and new business start-ups hang out dot.com shingles purporting to offer just such training and certification. By 2010, public schools and districts will be very aware of the need for individuals with deep understanding of IT and a strong ability to implement it, and we believe that it will be private enterprise, with some contributions by the districts themselves, that will meet the need.

FALSE STARTS

False starts over the past two decades have created a lingering doubt about the effectiveness or usefulness of IT for some educators. Network infrastructures that were poorly designed or badly underpowered failed to deliver Internet resources at a viable speed and in a reliable fashion when teachers did try to make use of it. Large investments in a particular platform have been wasted when the manufacturer abandoned it or when it was found to be incompatible with much of what was already in place. Products purchased as "low-bid" items were not manufactured to quality standards or were not designed with the classroom environment in mind and did not stand up past the first year of use. Software released before its time contained bugs that kept teachers struggling with system reboots and trying to install temporary fixes, and this interfered with teaching and learning and cost valuable contact time with students. In short, the technology has not been stable long enough to build confidence among users and potential users. The rapid rate of change for IT hardware and communications protocols creates instability, and so too does the premature release of a major piece of educational software, content specific or management, that has not been adequately tested and debugged. Businesses have learned to live in such a nonperfect world, but educators have shown little patience with those who promise much and deliver little.

TECHNOLOGY PLANNING

It is a long-standing maxim in educational technology circles that the district or school technology plan is a key to the success of technology utilization. It is almost heresy to question the wisdom of planning, but, nevertheless, planning without understanding what is at the cutting or bleeding edge of the field (hardware, software, protocols, standards, practices, etc.) can easily create a false start for a school or district. Too many plans have proceeded without insight about IT and its full potential for school environments. The notion that if one gets all the stakeholders together and gives them a voice in the plan, everything will proceed smoothly has been a fallacy from the outset. Such plans have had limited or no vision, and they often reflected the technology of last year rather than the technology that would actually be available two years down the road when the plan could finally be implemented.

Many educators sensed and admitted their lack of expertise in these areas and openly sought consultation with other educators and with industry experts. Unfortunately, the experts from outside did not (and still do not) understand the educational enterprise and often ended up misleading those they sought to serve. There has been no shortage of "experts" ready and willing to help schools with technology planning and infrastructure. The problem is that they have little of value to help educators with their particular tasks. To a large extent, K–12 educators have tried to move forward with bad advice from industry experts, with no help from their colleagues in higher education, and with no assistance from either the state or the federal government, which continues to want to "study the problem."

The proliferation of conferences and workshops around educational technology was an amazing thing to watch during the 1980s and continues even into the twenty-first century. Educational technology conferences have become a major industry unto themselves. K–12 educators who have been successful have had to learn how to read the industry and develop very sensitive "crap" detectors. Successes have come only after a long process of trial and error, a practice that is still in wide use. Even today, one can find conflicting "expert" advice on topics related to educational technology and its use. How about wireless technologies? Are they viable yet? Should we take fiber to the desktop in classrooms or stay with Category 5 copper? Should we switch to Category 6 for our cabling plant? Which platform is best suited for K–12 school use? Can students become proficient or fluent in IT based on the amount of exposure they receive as teachers integrate it into traditional courses of study? Does IT deserve its own place in the curriculum as part of fundamental literacy in the twenty-first century? Questions such as these fuel hot debates during the development of technology plans, and eventually the loudest voice or that deemed most authoritarian wins. The plan that results will or will not work. It is still a trial-and-error process for most. School and district technology plans are no guarantee of success, and much energy expended on plans could be better spent on pilot projects that inform and add to institutional knowledge about IT and its use in K–12 education.

ABSENCE OF STANDARDS AND
FAILURE TO ADHERE TO STANDARDS

The creation of and adherence to standards fuel IT successes. When the arrival of Open Systems Interconnections, or OSI standards for networking, were implemented on a wide scale, IT made major advances in the private sector. OSI represents a set of protocols and definitions that have provided international standardization of many aspects of computer-to-computer communications. Finally, with OSI, one is able to have a reasonable level of assurance that devices bought from different vendors will work when placed in the same infrastructure. Other standards deal with data structures and ensure that information stored in one database product can communicate with and be exchanged with data in another. Unfortunately, standards do not arrive fully developed at the time they are most needed. In educational settings, we continue to rely on OSI and a range of standards created by the Institute of Electrical and Electronics Engineers, Inc., but the world of computer and communications standards is a dynamic one. What is standard practice one year may be gone the next.

Database standards designed for the unique requirements of keeping student records have been slow to emerge. In 2001 there has been an effort to define such a standard, referred to as the Schools Interoperability Framework, or SIF. Initiated by Microsoft and now under the guidance of the Software and Information Industry Association, it is a blueprint for education software interoperability and data access. The SIF, if successfully implemented, will offer an open specification for ensuring that K–12 instructional and administrative software applications work together more effectively. Like OSI, SIF is not a product but, rather, an industry-supported blueprint. In this case, it sets specifications for K–12 education software that will enable diverse applications to interact and share data seamlessly. It is not difficult to see the advantages of such a standard. If it existed, data would only have to be entered once and then could be used freely by other applications. Also, it could facilitate the exchange of data among institutions and agencies to which they report.

Will the SIF initiative be successful? Only time will determine whether this data standard will be the one that moves educational data processing forward. Already there is a competing movement supported by the U.S. government to create a standard for data exchange, referred to as Electronic Data Interchange, or EDI. This is a standard that can make possible the almost instant transfer of information, regardless of what type of student information system a school district might use. EDI is a competing standard to SIF in 2001. It is designed to serve a separate purpose than the SIF standard and will not necessarily benefit the schools and districts themselves. Whereas SIF is vendor generated to let applications within a district communicate with each other, EDI is intended for transferring student records from district to district, from state to state, or from school district to college admissions offices. EDI is based on a long-standing data format referred to as X12, whereas SIF is based on a format referred to as XML, a more recent effort. At the moment, EDI is more mature than SIF.

Consequently, many groups already have a personal stake in EDI and the X12 format. Perhaps the two standards will be able to communicate with one another, but the necessity for them to do so will extend the implementation time. As with standards in other fields, the major problem is that there are so many of them. The continued evolution and adoption of standards in all aspects of IT are essential to K–12 adoption and use. The delay of standards will delay full integration and use. The prospect for standards is good, but the field will remain a dynamic one.

LEADERSHIP AND FEAR

In the absence of a clear vision of what is possible and where public education will go with IT, those in leadership positions have not embraced the real change in the practices and processes of schooling that IT affords. There is reluctance (perhaps fear) to move off the traditional path. Failure to understand translates into reluctance to make significant changes, and K–12 education atrophies. Teachers and administrators are themselves afraid of how IT might affect their work routines or their careers, and they are reluctant to move away from what have become comfortable routines in their classrooms and schools. IT has been added onto everything else that schools have been doing, and the necessity of dealing with it has increased the unnecessary burden on school staffs. Again, either through reluctance or fear, educators refuse to change traditional practices to accommodate new opportunities. A classic example of this lies in the traditional report card sent home to parents several times a year.

Teachers record grades for homework, tests, projects, and exams for each student and then somehow transform this into a letter or number grade for several weeks of study. Parents look at an A- or a number grade of 91 and think that they have an understanding of their child's performance. Consider the district that implemented a state-of-the-art instructional management system that allows teachers to record daily progress on each curriculum objective the child studies and annotate each child's record with personal comments. At any time a color graph with detailed comments that shows precisely how a child has been performing on any or all of the course objectives may be presented for a parent. These multiple-page and in-depth reports were sent home at the end of each grading period along with a traditional report card. When teachers complained about maintaining two separate grading systems, the district feared dropping the less meaningful report card in favor of the very detailed progress report. Would parents understand the new format? Would they accept it? Fear of change about something as simple as a report card format could doom what has been a very powerful implementation of IT in that district.

The public school experience with IT has not been in a depth or of a quality that reveals its true potential. Likewise, this limited experience factor has kept educators from realizing on a personal level the fact that the value of IT lies not simply in doing work more efficiently but, indeed, in changing how work is done. IT is most effective when it helps people do their work better. In school settings the people in question are students (first and foremost), and their job is learning. Perhaps schools will have to go around teachers directly to the students. By equipping students with personal computers to use on-line and digital resources stored on their hard drives, they may begin to realize the full benefits of technology.

Schools are still throwing money at technology instead of working strategically to infuse technology into the fundamental processes of schooling. Schools have paid lip service to IT but continue to keep it at a distance, burying it behind the attempt to integrate it with the stuff that "really counts."

What has been called business process integration in the private sector has yet to come to public education. As the distinction between computing and communication has faded, IT's impact in business and the military has been to facilitate a transition from functional organizational structures to process-aligned organizations that can take advantage of the strategic value of information as it flows within the enterprise. The notion of "intelligent enterprises" is not new by any means, but public education has shown little interest in the concept to date. In an "intelligent" or "smart" public school, all stakeholders (especially parents and students) have access to the right information at the right time and in a format that suits their needs and level of understanding. Information informs all decisions. Bad decisions and actions are analyzed to determine what information misled the decision makers. Once the mistake or bad information is identified, the "system" is modified so that it will be more accurate in the future. In short, the enterprise is a learning organization, one that recognizes the systematic nature of its business and behaves accordingly.

FAILURE TO CONSIDER TOTAL COST OF OWNERSHIP OR RETURN ON INVESTMENT AND ADJUST PLANS AND ACTIONS ACCORDINGLY

School technology plans usually state a vision and outline a level of IT resources to be implemented and a schedule for doing so. School boards are reluctant not to support technology plans because they have a notion that it is very important to have IT in their schools. The news is full of stories about new technologies and the many high-tech jobs that are going unfilled. Sadly, neither school boards and administrators nor the public who votes on bond referendums for technology understand the concepts of "return on investment" (ROI) or "total cost of ownership"

(TCO). Consequently, technology plans get bogged down very quickly around issues of maintenance, support, training, and replacement cycles.

Based on a trend analysis conducted by the Gartner Group, since 1987 the five-year TCO in the private sector (including equipment and training) usage and maintenance of a DOS-based PC ballooned from $19,296 to $41,536. This is an increase of 153 percent! That translates to an annual cost of $8,307 per computer. The Gartner study can be found on-line at the time of this writing at the following URL: http://www.guardianinfo.com/industry/industry.htm. Cost factors that contribute to TCO are illustrated in figure 4.2.

The TCO in education is about one-half this amount, for schools have lower levels of technical support. But even at half the costs of ownership at the private level, the cost to implement IT in K–12 schools usually far exceeds the expectations of planners.

Local boards and state legislatures are beginning to ask about their ROI from IT over the past decade, and results are mixed. Technology plans usually have no provision for demonstrating total value of ownership (TVO) of IT resources. Without hard data documenting TVO, funding will continue to be unpredictable. With extremely high costs for purchase and installation and the added cost of supporting these resources, public schools will continue to struggle to find adequate financing for IT. Change will require courageous leadership to break from traditional practices on many fronts and allow IT to replace traditional resources and processes. It will take strategic use of IT to defray costs across the process of schooling before its use can be sustained over the long term. Public schools are

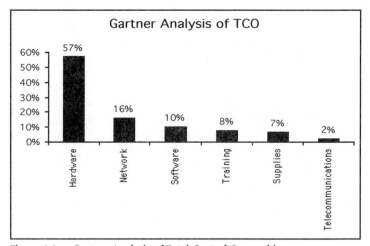

Figure 4.2.   Gartner Analysis of Total Cost of Ownership

learning this very slowly, and by 2010 we believe that the trends toward structural change should become apparent.

COMPLEXITY OF USING IT IN EDUCATIONAL SETTINGS

Achieving anything like full utilization of IT in public education is not a simple task. The very nature of public education complicates the use of IT on every front. Every group that has involved itself in the process of transferring technology to education has underestimated the scope of the task. This includes researchers, planners, state and federal governments, and the IT industry itself. The federal government is especially culpable in terms of its inability to provide direction and support for strategic initiatives. With federal initiatives like EDI, which competes head-on with the industry's own SIF, a case can be made that the federal government is itself an obstacle to progress.

A Native American saying helps illustrate the problem of full utilization of IT by schools: "The fox knows many small things, but the ground hog knows one big thing. What the ground hog knows is that you can't change just one thing." Indeed, unless public education re-creates itself around the capabilities afforded by information technologies, the investments being made in infrastructure and programs are unlikely to produce anything like the results that other institutions have experienced. Programs and strategies that add IT as another layer to what is already traditional practice are destined to failure in the long term. If IT is used appropriately and to the fullest advantage, as it should be, everything about K–12 education will change.

THE MISSING CHIEF INFORMATION OFFICER

Business and industry came to grips with the need for comprehensive management of IT within their organizations and created a new top-level executive position, the chief information officer or CIO. The primary role that has emerged for the CIO has been to come to grips with the big picture. Successful CIOs are individuals who know IT and understand the role that IT has assumed in the modern world. Further, the successful CIO knows the business of the organization intimately—all its processes and products. The CIO has become the change agent for many institutions and leads them through a process of reinventing themselves as knowledge-based institutions.

Public education has not produced IT leadership from within comparable to what other institutions have accomplished. Even when executive-level positions are established for IT in school districts or state departments of education, it is likely that those who fill them will not come from the business side of education, the classroom, or even from frontline district administration. They are more likely to be university, government, or industry data-processing retreads who have little understanding of the business of public education.

The prospect for improvement on the leadership front is not good for the near or midterm. Neither institutions of higher education nor school districts themselves are investing in training and development for IT leadership. The question is, Where do you find individuals with leadership potential who have a deep understanding of human learning and of the challenges facing public education who also possess a solid background in IT? Leadership to guide education through the transformation process will have to evolve over the long term, or the IT industry itself will be in the driver's seat in terms of how schools use technology. Indeed, without leadership, schools and districts may not be in a position to compete with learning services that will be offered by the commercial sector. The looming challenge to K–12 schools from new learning service providers is discussed more fully in chapter 5.

FALSE PROPHETS AND JUDAS GOATS

Education technology has had its share of pundits and prophets who have predicted everything from the end of schooling as we know it to a new system of public education that "is right around the corner," something promised since the computer was first conceived. Others have been quick to sell schools on turnkey solutions "guaranteed" to solve every problem from low standardized test scores to teacher shortages. Of course, technology has not yet proven itself as a panacea, nor is it likely to in the near- or midterm future. Significant progress will be slow in coming, and many blind alleys and dead-end paths will appear along the way.

Public educators have been "sitting ducks" in their vulnerability to high pressure and the very slick sales techniques used on them. So-called visionaries have misled many districts deep into untried and unproven applications that inevitably failed and left them having to start all over again. In his book, *Zen and the Art of Motorcycle Maintenance*,[5] Robert Pirsig calls these missteps "gumption traps." Falling into a gumption trap takes the wind out of one's sails, and the next effort has to be even greater than the first just to overcome the inertia that the trap inevitably brings with it. The institution of K–12 education must fully develop institutional knowledge to be able to see through the hype to what is real and to avoid dead ends and traps of all kinds.

TEACHER TRAINING HYPE

We believe that the failure of schools to more fully utilize IT has its roots in places other than inadequate teacher training. It is true that school-based personnel continue to ignore IT for the most part and have relatively few IT skills beyond word processing or the most basic applications. We also believe that no amount of training of teachers already in service will overcome this reluctance. More important to the future uses of IT in schools is how the leadership of schools and districts responds to the opportunities that IT affords.

The leadership of boards of education, superintendents, and directors of instruction have themselves not incorporated IT into their own personal and work lives. Consequently, they cannot recognize the opportunities that IT affords them for improving their own productivity, let alone the more relevant IT applications for schools, when they encounter them. Technology planning is typically left to select individuals in the schools and in the central office. Those in charge of planning know pretty well what the limits of change are and keep within them. Even where insightful IT users in schools do exist, the system as defined by those above continues to limit the range of what schools attempt to do with IT.

Much more progress in assimilating IT into school practices will come from in-depth training and experience for the top levels of school leadership than will come from unlimited spending on teacher and principal training. Contrary to popular belief, we do not believe that the school principal is the key to full integration of IT. Rather, we believe that the board members and the superintendent and central staff are more critical. It is they who set limits, stated and unstated. It is they who are in a position to implement projects that change traditional practices in favor of new ones. It is they who define operations and procedures that become the culture of the school and district, and it is they who must lead efforts at change.

Superintendents may be reluctant because of the limited knowledge of board members (public school boards and private school boards of directors). As we discuss in later chapters, schools represent more than places to learn content. They have social value beyond academic learning and test scores, and boards are reluctant to tamper with processes that their publics have come to understand and expect. Something as simple as changing the way in which grades are reported can be the subject of parental complaint and revolt. Changes in school schedules for the day or year can really agitate a community. Too many educational leaders have not been willing to take the risk to make even small changes in traditional practice.

As consumers of school services begin to expect schools to make changes, more will be willing to attempt them. When and if school leaders become more enlightened about IT and how other institutions use it, perhaps they will take at least some moderate degree of risk and implement procedural changes that will leave no wiggle room for school staffs. Once the need to become fluent in information technology is felt, teachers and school-based administrators will develop their skills and get on with it. Just as there is truth in the belief that teaching is not required for learning to take place, so it is true that staff development is not required for adults to become fluent with IT. IT fluency is just another learning task, and it is not a difficult one at that. Learning is and always will be something one has to do for oneself. People learn when they are interested and when there is clear need to learn.

NOTES

1. Software and Information Industry Association, *Building the Net: Trends Report 2000* (July 2000). Available at http://www.trendsreport.net/summary/summary.html.

2. U.S. Office of Technology Assessment, *Teachers and Technology: Making the Connection,* GPO stock #052-003-01409-2, Government Printing Office (April 1995), 2. Available at ftp://otabbs.ota.gov/pub/teachers.tech.

3. The CEO Forum on Education and Technology, *Teacher Preparation StaR Chart: A Self-Assessment Tool for Colleges of Education* (January 2000), 1.

4. American Association of Colleges for Teacher Education, "Alternative Certification: A Position Statement of AACTE," *Journal of Teacher Education* 36, no. 3 (1986): 24.

5. Robert M. Pirsig, *Zen and the Art of Motorcycle Maintenance* (New York: Bantam Books, 1984).

5

The Near-Term Future of Technology in Education: 2001–07

From their early introduction, computer and communications technologies created new expectations for improving the quality and controlling the cost of K–12 education. As discussed in previous chapters, the difficulties encountered in realizing these expectations have far exceeded what most ever anticipated. Information technology is by its nature in a constant state of change and quite complex in its structure. Schools themselves are more complex places than most recognize. It is the failure to understand and accommodate the complexity and the dynamics of both schools and IT that presents the biggest obstacle to the full implementation of IT in education. The limited success that education has enjoyed to date speaks to the difficulty of the challenge, but it is clear that whatever the challenge, there will be growing use of and dependence on IT in the future of K–12 education. In the remainder of the book, we consider what present trends suggest about this future. We look at the future through three windows, the near term (2001–07), the midterm (2008–14), and the longer term (2015–21). There is nothing magical about these dates. We selected them because they represent the blocks of time that have pretty much defined the rate at which new technology has been introduced into education. For example, once the personal computer arrived on the marketplace in 1977, it took about six years for schools to begin to adopt them in significant numbers. Likewise, after networks became fashionable toward the end of the 1980s, schools were pretty much gearing up to install them by 1993.

2001–07

In the near-term future, schools will continue to struggle with the basics of IT and learning how to utilize various tools and resources. We begin this period with a large inventory of outdated legacy hardware and software. Many network infrastructures from the early to mid-1990s frequently cannot do the job asked of them today. Some hardware and software resources now used in K–12 schools are older than ten years. Legacy resources introduced as recently as three or four years ago are proving inadequate to accommodate the more sophisticated uses schools will be attempting in the near term. Much of the networking completed in the 1990s has already proven that it is inadequate to handle growing traffic around use of the Internet's multimedia resources and locally stored digital materials. It is common in 2001 at technology conferences to hear IT directors bemoaning the need to rip out older 10b2, Thicknet, and Token Ring networks to install switched gigabit Ethernet. Technology plans developed during the 1990s too often failed to provide for timely replacement cycles for hardware and software, even after it was realized by many that IT would become integral to the day-to-day operations of schools. As a result, public education will spend most of the period between 2001 and 2007 adjusting plans, improving infrastructures, replacing legacy resources, and implementing processes to better accommodate the realities of what IT demands once it becomes fundamental to the K–12 enterprise.

Adjustments and upgrades to infrastructures and IT components will come at a time when the private sector is learning to work more effectively with the K–12 education market. In the private sector economy, what started as a business-to-business model quickly became a business-to-customer model, a pattern that will likely repeat itself in education. Thus, while schools busy themselves with IT details and upgrading their resources, they are likely to lose at least a portion of their traditional services to commercial providers.

The period 2001–07 will see the introduction of many new and improved technologies and resources along with new techniques for integrating them into the processes of operating schools. There is no shortage of critics asking whether schools, as diverse as they are in terms of readiness and understanding of the forces at work, can position themselves to compete with the emerging new class of learning organizations. Beyond 2007, the competition will begin to gain momentum, and schools will recognize that they do have serious competition for students. Whether K–12 schools will survive the competition that is taking shape on the Web and gaining momentum through private efforts to redefine how people learn is a question that we will come back to several times in the rest of this book. In effect, K–12 education enters the period 2001–07 with the dual task of dealing with the physical components of IT while also adjusting its vision and redesigning its procedures and professional practices.

PHYSICAL FACTORS, 2001–07

There are major physical factors schools will have to deal with effectively if they hope to retain all of the services they now provide their communities. The need to renetwork and to establish funding for four-year replacement cycles for computers and peripherals has come as a surprise to boards of education of public schools, boards of directors of private schools, and state departments of education that have assumed that the billions already spent on IT have positioned them to move forward with relative ease. "Where did all that money go," they ask? "Were networks not installed in our schools? Didn't we train our teachers how to use these tools ten years ago?" Yes, we did install networks and we did train extensively. What we installed and the way we trained do not meet the new uses and expectations for the use of IT. Times change, and so does technology.

In the absence of specifications and standards about how to network and how to implement IT during the last two decades of the twentieth century, schools spent their funds and their efforts largely in a process of trial and error. A lot of it, as it turns out, was in error. On a positive note, however, what K–12 education has learned from the trial-and-error period will enable it to enter the twenty-first century with more insight and understanding about what needs to be done and how to go about it. In this sense, the money spent on IT in K–12 schooling since the early 1980s has paid a dividend in terms of the institutional knowledge it has generated. With prices for IT components coming down, and assuming continued level or slightly increased funding for IT, schools should be able to get themselves into shape much more quickly and with less expense than the first time around. For example, a 500 megahertz multimedia computer can be purchased today for about $600. This is a fully configured machine with a 10/100 Ethernet network card, DVD drive, monitor, keyboard, sound card, ten gb or larger hard drive, and at least sixty-four mb of memory. A similarly configured computer would have cost more than $2,500 three years ago.

The computer itself will continue to evolve keeping within the principles of Moore's Law. The three major trends in the evolution of the personal computer are that it is getting faster, smaller, and cheaper. Already, processor speeds of 1.5 gigahertz (1.5 billion operations per second) are coming out of test furnaces in the chip factories. Having said that, however, processor speed itself is likely to have minimal impact on education technology in the near term. Software to take advantage of today's processing speeds has not and is not coming out of development. The software component for K–12 education seems to be the more difficult of the variables to define and produce, and the lack of appropriate software will limit the impact of IT on schools during the near term.

Of all the variables, the fact that computers are getting smaller and cheaper will have the most impact in the near term. As prices reach the $300 level, schools will be able to reduce student-to-computer ratios such that digital resources can begin to replace traditional ones. Replaced items will likely include most textbooks, calculators, and paper-based library reference materials. Through replacing these items rather than supplementing them with a small amount of IT, more funds will be available for IT resources. It is very likely that as 2007 nears, we will find many schools across the United States in which each student is issued a personal digital device with all the functions one finds in a good laptop computer today. There are school districts today that are providing each student with a personal laptop computer in grades 6–12. This trend will continue and expand. Achievement of a one-to-one student-to-computer ratio is likely to come first to the high school grades, 9 through 12, and then move down to grade 5 or 6. The prospect of a one-to-one ratio is significantly enhanced by the growing popularity and functionality of small devices such as the Palm Pilot, Compaq's pocket computer, and Apple's new iBook laptop. Whereas the iBook has the right feature set, the Palm Pilot comes closer to the price range needed to make the devices ubiquitous.

eBOOKS

Another development that will facilitate the role of the broad use of small, low-cost digital devices for learning is the effort to develop standards for electronic books. eBooks, as they have come to be called, are one of the newer digital appliances coming to market. The eBook promises to have a wide-reaching effect on the publishing industry similar to the effect that video had on the film industry. eBook proponents argue with good cause that they will change the way we read.

An eBook, sometimes called a reader, is a small handheld device with limited functionality. It is primarily a storage and display unit. One of the models on the market in 2001 is the Rocket eBook, which plugs into a cradle that attaches to a personal computer. The computer accesses electronic book sites on the Web, from which text can be loaded into the eBook via the computer hookup. Some prototypes offer a modem to enable the user to download textbooks or novels directly to the eBook from Web-based publishers, a group that is growing in number each year. For a list of eBook publishers, check the following URL: http://www.itl.nist.gov/div895/ebook2000/info.html.

The Open eBook Forum (OEBF) is a group dedicated to the creation of standards that will promote the successful adoption of electronic books and maintain consistency among the devices that allow one to read them. If OEBF is successful, the IT industry will assimilate an association of hardware and software companies, publishers, authors, and users of electronic books and related organizations. Already there is evidence that the public is enthusiastic about and accepting of the emerging electronic publishing industry. One can follow the evolution of and the debate around eBooks at the OEBF website at http://www.openebook.org.

The Kansas State Library System maintains a site on the World Wide Web that monitors the experiments going on today with eBooks. The site is found at http://skyways.lib.ks.us/central/ebooks/libraries.html. A quick look at the projects listed there will show that interest among libraries in eBook technology is strong. Within the publishing industry itself, companies are positioning themselves for a strong presence in the eBook market as it develops between 2001 and 2007. By 2007, the eBook could be as common as printed books in many curriculum areas, especially with college and high school textbooks, most notably those that have the least need for multimedia content.

A possible role for faster CPU speeds and cheaper dynamic memory chips will be their use in eBooks designed to handle texts that incorporate multimedia components such as sound, video, and graphics. When such devices are available at prices between $100 and $200, traditional printed textbooks are likely to pass into history. They will simply be too expensive compared with the electronic alternatives, and, very likely, most curriculum content will not be available in printed form—only in electronic form. We expect eBooks to be firmly established by 2007 and to make a major contribution to the integration of IT into public education.

Whether schools will utilize separate devices for calculating, communicating, and storing electronic books remains to be seen. At the moment, the market is uncertain about how digital appliances will evolve. As we near 2007, we feel that it is likely that different devices will be used for different functions such as graphing calculators, eBooks, laptops, and geographical information devices. eBooks themselves will evolve first as separate devices, but as the IT industry consolidates between 2008 and 2014, different functions will be assimilated into powerful, small, portable digital devices capable of supporting a wide array of input, storage, display, and communication peripherals. These devices will cost between $200 and $500 per student. That price will also include productivity software and, perhaps, bundled digital content licenses. While that may seem like a large sum of money to spend on individual students for IT, the real cost has to take into account savings on items being replaced. We believe that the overall cost of providing educational content and resource materials will be no more in 2007 than it is in 2001 and may perhaps be slightly less.

NETWORK INFRASTRUCTURES AND MOBILE COMPUTING

Network infrastructures will be undergoing significant change during the near term as well. Nonscaleable topologies that were adopted because they were cheap to install at the time must be replaced. Shared, ten-megabit networks simply will not support the intensive traffic placed on local and wide-area infrastructures. Technology-intensive schools struggling with ten-megabit networks today can attest to their limitations. As recently as 1998, it was commonly thought that servers that would "fill the network pipeline" were distant, and investments in ten-megabit infrastructures seemed a safe bet. Streaming video and multiple multimedia applications soon dispelled any thought that ten megabits would suffice.

Migration from shared ten-megabit networks to switched ten-megabit and then switched 100-megabit infrastructures will be swift during the period 2001–07. Schools that have benefited from funding from the e-Rate program have come to rely on Internet resources to support instruction, and that dependency will grow each year. The search for scaleable network protocols and topologies will continue for the foreseeable future. Quite simply, there will never be enough bandwidth to meet the need. Whatever capacity is created will quickly be filled.

The evolution of networks will not be limited to their carrying capacity, however. Schools are beginning to discover the advantages of mobile computing, and these advantages are such that mobile computing will be in wide use even before 2007. Mobile computing utilizes battery-operated and wirelessly networked laptop or portable computers. This combination immediately solves several obstacles that face educators trying to integrate IT into their programs. The first is space. Small portable devices are less intrusive in the traditional classroom. They can be kept out of the way until they are needed, much as a textbook is today. Being battery operated, they do not require time or expense to provide additional electrical service to scores of classrooms in a school. Because they are wirelessly networked, the need for intrusive cables that lie underfoot or exposed wires and conduit tubes clamped to classroom walls is eliminated. Also, adding wireless hubs to an existing hardwired infrastructure is a quick and relatively inexpensive way to expand an existing network's capabilities.

In June 1997, the Institute of Electrical and Electronic Engineers (IEEE) completed the standard for wireless local area networks (LANs), referred to as IEEE 802.11. In late 1999, the institute published two supplements to its initial 802.11 standard. These were 802.11a and 802.11b. The 802.11b standard operates in the 2.4 GHz band, but data rates can be as high as eleven mb. (So does the initial 802.11 standard.) These developments have opened the door for products to come to market that allow digital devices to communicate at eleven megabits per second (mbps), although the actual throughput is closer to ten mbps. The 802.11a standard specifies operation in the 5.8 GHz band with data rates that can go up to forty mbps. The advantages of this standard are its much higher carrying capacity and less radio frequency interference with other types of devices such as wireless telephones. At the time of this writing, it seems that 802.11a products will be available as early as late summer 2001. These devices are reported to provide a thirty-three mb throughput. It is important that we acknowledge the 802.11a standard to illustrate that wireless topologies will continue to scale just as hardwired networks have been doing for decades.

The advantages that schools have identified for wireless LANs include more efficient use of space and more productivity. Productivity in this case is defined as more utilization of an IT resource once it is purchased. Wireless LANs may actually enable some schools to buy fewer computers. Because they are not in fixed locations and frequently inaccessible because non-computer-using classes occupy the rooms where they are located, mobile machines, theoretically at least, can be used more often. However, the call for a one-to-one student-to-computer ratio may offset this cost advantage. A mobile IT resource can be more easily moved within a room as well as between rooms or labs. In this way, the mobile resource has a better fit for more instructional strategies than the traditional approach that places desktop computers hardwired to the network in a corner of the room. Teachers are more likely to adopt mobile devices as part of their repertoire of tools because they are less physically intrusive and more easily incorporated into classroom activities.

Wireless LANs also promise to be relatively inexpensive on a per-student basis, and very fast and easy installation is possible. Running cable through ceilings and walls has always been costly, and the process runs the risk of disturbing asbestos insulation that will at the very least force a costly removal process and at worst can risk exposing staff and students to harmful substances. From early adopters of mobile computing, it is reported that users can expect an increase in reliability of their networks. Hardwired cable plants have many metal and fiber connections that can either corrode or be interfered with by remodeling or vandalism. Simply, there are more potential points of failure in hardwired infrastructures. The wireless LAN is simpler with fewer components and, hence, is more reliable.

The wireless communication revolution is bringing fundamental changes to data networking, just as it already has to voice telecommunications. By freeing the end user from the wire and a fixed position, digital devices become more flexible and more useful. In summary, the advantages of mobile computing in schools cover a broad spectrum that includes the following:

- mobility
- lower cost
- easier to install in difficult-to-wire areas

- increased reliability
- reduced installation time

The present limitation of wireless LANs to eleven megabits will result in their use occurring first in hybrid networks. Hybrid networks utilize a fiber or copper physical cabling plant as well as wireless access hubs or wireless access points strategically placed around the school. For many low-bandwidth applications, students and staff will use wireless connectivity. For higher bandwidth applications, they can connect to a network drop that offers more bandwidth at megabit or gigabit speeds. Schools that are building hybrid networks today are typically installing switched 100-megabit cable plants and providing clusters of wireless laptops to supplement desktop units. To function fully in a hybrid environment, the laptop or mobile computer should have both a wireless network card and a 100-megabit Ethernet card. When wireless devices are available at higher rates, the need for hardwired infrastructures will likely decrease until they are the exception rather than the rule. We are moving toward a wireless future, but that day for public schools is probably as late as 2007 or beyond.

The advantages of mobile computing also suggest that more affluent students will choose to own a laptop computer and bring it to school if one is not provided. This is a trend that is already evident across the United States. The advantage of having a personal computer in school full-time will bring more debate about the digital divide and prompt both federal and state legislators to provide funding for laptops for general student use. By 2007 local and state initiatives to reduce the digital divide will be common across the United States.

WIRELESS WIDE-AREA NETWORKS IN 2001

A technology called public key infrastructure, or PKI, is being experimented with in several communities across the United States. The township of Hamilton, New Jersey, for example, is attempting to bring wireless Internet access and other data services to the town's central business area. Trying to avoid the disruptions that fiber and copper cables create in communities when they are installed, Hamilton will utilize small transmitters, about the size of a loaf of bread, which are being placed on utility poles and streetlights around the town. This particular wireless technology claims data transfer speeds of up to 128 kilobits, slow by any standard. Hamilton is not alone in its efforts, as more than 400 communities across the United States are engaged in similar projects.

A key issue with PKI technology is who will bear the cost of installing and maintaining it. Another factor that has to be overcome before wireless connectivity offers serious challenges to physical cable plants is the connection speed. Perhaps the most important point about PKI technology is that enough has been done with it already to prove its functionality and reliability. Whether the present form of the technology takes us into the midterm future or another form evolves is not the point. Once engineers find ways to overcome a few limitations, wireless networking for voice, video, and data will become as pervasive as the telephone and the television.

Today's connection speed used by wireless network devices severely restricts what we can do with wireless devices when they are connected to wide-area networks or metropolitan-area networks. The devices we refer to here are not the laptop computers that work on the 801.11 Ethernet protocol discussed earlier. Rather, wireless in this sense refers to connecting remote sites or buildings in metropolitan-area and wide-area networks using radio waves. St. John's County, Florida, is aggressively installing these networks in the anticipation that transmission speeds over long distances will be fast enough to meet their needs once the networks themselves are in place. The technology we are using in 2001 is sometimes referred to as second-generation wireless and connects at a snail's pace compared with wired devices. The rates today fall between 9,600 bits per second and 14,400 bits per second. Some industry experts expect the "fabulous" speed of fifty-six Kb by 2002. That speed will allow some transfer of multimedia images from the Internet but will still be child's play compared with gigabit speeds of fiber connections. Third-generation wireless will be short lived, for the real goal lies in fourth-generation speeds that will appear around 2005–06 if the experts are on target with their forecasts. We wish St. John's County and others luck with their wireless efforts, but we cannot recommend them for long-range connectivity at this time.

In time there will be a range of educational applications of wide-area wireless technologies. As the connection speeds reach functional levels, wide-area wireless simply extends the metaphor of anywhere, anytime learning. Other applications, though far-fetched, may include monitoring the location of students based on global positioning systems (GPS). Student ID cards could contain small transmitters that would allow counselors or parents to locate a child within a few feet of a city street corner. Are they in school or skipping to play with friends? Small handheld computers available today could connect to wireless networks so students could download or access personal information such as addresses, collect assignments, or receive e-mail. The learning utility of such applications seem in no way comparable to the full-function personal computer with a broadband connection to the Internet, but the technology bears watching. Companies such as Palm are taking a serious interest in creating an education market for wireless handheld devices. Recording test scores, taking attendance, checking electronic ID cards, and other applications have been experimented with in several locations. At the moment, however, there is no large-scale trend indicating that handheld computers and palm-sized devices will replace the personal computer.

Some interesting devices are coming into the market, however. In addition to a wearable computer introduced by IBM, Intel is offering its Web Pad. The Web Pad is about the size of a pocketbook and offers wireless Internet access. Nokia and Nextel, among others, offer multifunction cell phones that double as two-way radio communication devices and offer wireless Internet access. Storage technology is increasing the functionality of these devices as well. Sony has introduced "memory stick" data storage devices that are about the size of a stick of chewing gum and presently can hold about sixty-four mb of digital information. The Palm VIIx we have used on occasion to take notes for this book offers wireless Internet access for news, weather, stock reports, and e-mail. Like other devices in the category, the Palm offers synchronization with our desktop electronic calendars, address books, and calculator and comes with options for GPS functions.

DIGITAL CONTENT

The movement toward digital content for learning that is already well under way will be gathering momentum throughout this period. With the merger of America Online (AOL) with Time Warner, another vast library of digital content will be available for delivery to school-, home-, and community-based users. The introduction of AOL@School in 2000 represents something of a milestone in the evolution toward reliance on digital content for learning. Offered free to schools, AOL@School is but one example of an emerging business-to-business and business-to-customer model of e-commerce in the K–12 education arena. Other companies also offer the same kind of material but not on the scale that AOL–Time Warner has the potential to offer.

Education portals such as AOL@School represent today's most common approach to providing digital content. Portal companies locate and link teachers and learners to Web-based content. At the same time, state departments of education and some local districts are building their own portals. Some are negotiating rights to publish electronic versions of textbooks for learners to use anywhere and anytime. To see an example of an education portal, visit Education Planet at http://www.educationplanet. com/. Like many such portals, Education Planet is offering a tutoring service from its site. Other examples include Lightspan, Inc., at http://www.lightspan.com and K–12 Video Interactive at http://www. k-12video.com. The latter provides streaming video clips directly over the

Internet. Video materials available on demand for teachers and learners are but one advantage of digital content over paper-based materials. To see examples of streaming video, go to the Learning Station at http://www.learningstation.com or to the USA Video Interactive, Inc., site at http://www.usvo.com. Advocates of increased use of streaming video make the claim that a visual environment contributes to higher test scores and helps students quickly gain an intuitive understanding of abstract concepts that ensures greater success in their formal studies. Available to the desktop on demand, streaming video content does eliminate many of the barriers to broader use of video materials for teaching and learning. Already established as a viable technology, video on demand will be a major teaching resource by 2007.

The advantages that digital content brings to the classroom ensure its broad adoption and use at school and at home or wherever learning takes place. What is not clear at this point is who will be providing access to the content. Will commercial services maintain server farms to house and deliver learning content? Many companies are already trying to assume strategic positions in that market, as we have noted. On the other hand, will regional education service centers such as those found in Texas, New York, and other states provide portal and content services to their schools? Some are considering doing so. Perhaps school districts themselves will assume control of the delivery of digital content, just as they have taken over other media in the past, for example, instructional videos over cable stations, video tapes, and video discs. The difficulty of creating interactive multimedia materials in the past would preclude all but the most capable school districts from creating, housing, and providing access to digital multimedia resources. However, as with most other IT areas, the creation of digital content is becoming easier all the time.

AUTHORING SYSTEMS

Courseware authoring systems have significantly reduced the time and resources needed to produce interactive digital content. Products such as Macromedia's *Web Learning Studio* provide relatively easy-to-use tools for creating interactive lessons. These tools allow the developer to provide built-in assessment and instructional management features. Management components of digital courseware will be an important feature as standards-based education becomes more entrenched into school culture by 2007. Good authoring packages enable users to create and deploy engaging, standards-based learning applications for delivery on the Web, across intranets, or via CD-ROMs. In the past, the production cost and the system requirements to run such programs effectively kept schools and school districts out of the development process. Today, with authoring product prices as low as $3,000 and the ability to develop courseware on typical Windows and Macintosh workstations, that constraint no longer exists. Lack of personnel time and expertise, however, continues to present obstacles to their use by schools and districts. The approach used by Blackboard, Inc., could help solve this problem. Blackboard offers the capability to design multimedia lessons and complete courses of study on the Internet complete with assessments and a comprehensive record management system. Blackboard's system even collects metadata that can be used in data-mining applications that a district might employ. Try you hand at developing an on-line lesson at the Blackboard website, located at http://www.blackboard.com.

We believe that schools and districts will rely initially on commercial providers of digital content, including streaming video. Smaller districts especially have limited capabilities for local development. Reliance on commercial providers for the long term, however, will present public education with limited options to what are already high prices for access and license fees. The use of advertisements on portal websites may be offered as one way to offset the cost to the districts, but this model is not working as well as anticipated. Internet-filtering company N2H2 announced in late 2000 that it would discontinue its free filtering service based on advertising placed in its banner at the bottom of the screen. Another possibility being investigated today has content providers selling market data they glean from the on-line behavior of their users (what sites they visit, what topics they have explored, etc.) in lieu of user fees. While these offers might seem attractive at first, in the future access to school district customer data may not be supported by the public or by state or local legislation. We do not believe that these financing approaches represent sustainable business models. Also, depending on market forces to create and maintain reliable long-term access to digital content may not be in the best interests of K–12 education. The market makes no guarantees about what it will do tomorrow in terms of its interest in the market or its pricing structure.

Larger districts, regional service centers, and consortia of smaller districts are likely to explore the potential of becoming content providers themselves. Some districts with the technical staff and server capacity may even host services for other less capable districts and end up in direct competition with commercial providers. Just as some school districts are in the business of providing distance learning services via satellite or switched digital video systems, so will the more entrepreneurial ones become adept at producing and marketing digital content over the Internet.

We believe that by 2007 a large number of digital content providers and provider types will be actively mining the K–12 education market. Large players will be the likes of Disney, AOL, traditional publishing houses, and even the Public Broadcasting Station. Anyone with a sizeable library of multimedia and text materials or access to the same will be capable of providing content. Many small Web-based portal or content provider companies will come and go in the near term. Just as the shakeouts have already come in the hardware and operating system markets, the digital content field will be reduced over time to the most comprehensive and most reliable providers, some of which, we believe, will be public school districts and consortia of districts.

WHAT ABOUT TEXTBOOKS DURING THE NEAR-TERM FUTURE?

While the period 2001–07 will be marked by the creation of digital content for learning on several fronts, the end of the dominance of the printed textbook will not occur until later. The remaining infrastructure needs of K–12 schools will keep the need for printed materials alive in most places. Wireless connectivity will help but not completely meet the need. At the same time, schools will require more time to develop efficient procedures to select and incorporate digital content into distributed learning experiences and into classroom-based lessons.

E-LEARNING

Another trend that will have a large impact on the near-term future of K–12 education is e-learning. Since the early days of the computer network, the dream of anyone being able to learn anything at anytime and at any place has remained a dream. e-Learning is sometimes referred to as distributed learning. The Internet now enables distributed learning to be made available to the masses. Distributed learning should be differentiated from distance learning. Distance learning commonly refers to the student, teacher, and other classmates being separated by some distance from one another. Distance learning courses have long been delivered via correspondence schools, by satellite, and by switched digital video networks. Many of these are synchronous in nature, but they can be asynchronous as well. Traditionally, distance learning courses are developed to fit time frames and lesson blocks that parallel traditional classroom instruction.

Distributed learning is a type of distance learning and refers to the ability of computer networks to connect learners, teachers, subject matter experts, and learning content, all of which may be dispersed around the globe. A traditional classroom teacher may have students communicate via e-mail in lieu of some class meetings and may provide learning material directly to the students by having them log on to his or her website. On the other hand, the strategy may be to send the student to a Web resource housed in a museum, a government office, or another school. The ingredients that traditionally were brought together into a self-contained classroom with four walls may now be located anywhere there is Web access.

Distributed learning techniques can be used to limit busing students to special programs within a district. Because everyone and everything the class needs can be accessed on the network, including the teacher, the need for transportation is eliminated, at least part of the time. Distributed learning may enable schools with limited demand for a high-level physics class, for example, to place students into the hands of a teacher in another school or in another district and thereby expand curriculum and contain personnel costs. While initial production costs are much higher, the delivery costs for e-learning techniques are far lower than those for traditional instructor-based classroom instruction. In addition, it has been estimated that technology-based strategies speed up the learning process by a factor of 20 to 80 percent, depending on the learner, the subject matter, and the design of the lesson.

Another factor that will rapidly drive e-learning comes from the changing nature of the workplace and the workforce. When and where people want and need to learn are not like they used to be. Working adults and adolescents no longer have time to take weeks, months, or even full days out of their work schedules to go to a school building to learn. Even in secondary education, many students work day jobs, and, increasingly, they need to be able to learn what they need when they need it without being at school. The anytime and anywhere model fits the changing needs of working students very well.

Simultaneously, what students need to learn, the curriculum, is expanding. The school day and the school year are not. Consequently, people need to learn more efficiently or learn at a faster pace or in patterns other than what the traditional classroom allows. e-Learning by its nature can better accommodate the fact that some people do not learn well in a structured, time-sensitive classroom and curriculum, and they sometimes require repetition and review to learn at all. Individual tutoring in classrooms of twenty-five to thirty-five has never been practical, but e-learning has the capacity to provide more support to learners who need it at the time they need it. Some people need more time to learn something than others do, and traditional classroom environments do not easily accommodate their needs.

Successful e-learning experiences will provide a rich multimedia environment that includes elements such as video, graphics, and animation as well as interactive simulations. Early successes with e-learning are beginning to come from hybrid approaches that combine traditional classroom instruction and e-learning. e-Learning tools, techniques, and resources empower the learner and supplement human instruction. As noted, the primary obstacle for schools and districts to develop their own e-learning materials lies in the absence of available personnel time and expertise to develop or use them. We will discuss this element more fully in the next section on differentiated staffing.

Whatever the source, e-learning very likely will be the great equalizer of the twenty-first century. When barriers of time, distance, and socioeconomic status are removed, individuals will be able to take charge of their own learning throughout life. We believe that by 2007, e-learning will be firmly established and e-learning providers will be challenging traditional schools and districts for their students. However, the greatest period of growth for e-learning will be the period 2008–14. For more on e-learning, search the Web or check out *e-Learning Magazine* at http://www.elearningmag.com/index.htm.

STAFF DEVELOPMENT

Experts and pundits alike have long touted professional development as the key to better use of IT in schools. Grants usually come with the proscription that a certain percentage of the funds be dedicated to teacher training. School and district technology planners are continuously admonished to ensure adequate training opportunities if they expect to succeed. We believe, based on extensive personal experience, that technology can be integrated into instruction without a great deal of staff development. Most teachers we have talked to freely acknowledged that training for them has been virtually useless. In spite of that, they continue to endorse district, state, and even federal plans that mandate professional development as a requirement for every project. Their motives are the additional pay to attend training and the opportunity to be away from students for a day or two, not the opportunity to develop IT skills.

Skilled IT-using educators get that way through their own initiative. They feel a need to know and to be more productive, and they have developed the sense that learning to be inventive and creative with these tools is vital to their professional future. Such motivation and understanding are all that is required to become a skilled technology-using educator. Staff development efforts would be better directed to these goals. The best and brightest are teaching themselves, just as their students are, but administrators and legislators continue the practice of "infantilizing" teachers. Those educators who have made a personal commitment to learn about IT and to do things differently do not have long to wait. Change will bring many new opportunities, and they will begin to arrive in various forms toward the end of this period.

We believe that the near-term future will bring more pressure on schools to be both more effective and more efficient. This pressure will eventually lead to significant redefinition of what schools' primary missions are and how they operate. Some have held this belief for decades, but the culture of schools has been able to successfully resist real paradigm shifts. What we are learning from the e-learning techniques being used today offers clues to one major area of change that will begin late in the near-term period. The current model of instructional delivery that places a teacher (subject matter expert) into a classroom and brings groups of learners before him or her to be taught certainly is not efficient, and more and more its effectiveness is being called into question. The e-learning movement is demonstrating how effective and efficient new paradigms can be, and they could finally lead to a change in the culture and practice of schooling in America.

Consider the time and effort that normally goes into the production of one well-planned and well-delivered lesson in a traditional school setting. The knowledge content of the lesson is first selected and probably tied to a state or local learning standard. Then the particular knowledge content must be organized in a fashion suited to the audience being asked to learn it. Teaching and learning materials are identified, located, and assembled. Supplemental materials to enrich, supplement, and, perhaps, broaden the scope of the content are also located and assembled. Tests and other informal assessments have to be prepared. Finally, first period arrives, and the teacher delivers the lesson for the first time. Second period comes around, and the teacher delivers a slightly better version of the lesson because of the practice afforded by the first teaching of the lesson. The third period class gets a pretty good version of the lesson as well, perhaps the best. By fourth period, the routine of repeating the lesson takes the edge off the teacher's delivery. If there are fifth and sixth periods, as frequently happens, the teacher has tired both physically and mentally, and the delivery leaves much to be desired by third period standards. The learner's schedule actually influences the quality of the lesson he or she receives.

Remember, this is but one teacher teaching one section of the course. The same content has been organized, developed, and taught by several teachers in the same building at essentially the same time. There may be as many as ten different senior English teachers planning and delivering lessons on *Julius Caesar* in any given high school. Approaches to instruction will vary according to the skills and preferences of the instructor. In terms of productivity, the same lesson was developed repeatedly by as many teachers as teach the subject in the school or in the district. The experience for students is quite variable, depending on the draw of teacher and the hour the student takes the class. The quality of the experience will also depend on how many different courses a teacher must prepare each day.

This routine is repeated each day, for new lessons have to be forthcoming on a daily basis. The time available to devote to developing one lesson is quite limited for a given teacher. This grinding routine causes teachers to go in search of the ready-made lesson in textbooks, on websites, or at conferences and workshops. Getting enough material to get through the class period each day is the biggest challenge for teachers in traditional school settings. It is easy to see how the traditional classroom actually prevents creative teaching. With four, six, or eight periods in the school day, there simply is not enough time. The one thing teachers always ask to have more of is planning time. They hate to be taken from planning and preparation to attend staff development or faculty meetings. If they do not have time to get enough "stuff" pulled together during school hours, they will have to do it on their own time. It is not uncommon to find teachers working until well into the evening hours at schools across the country. With such a model, teacher burnout is assured, and mediocre quality is about all one can expect. Yet it is the prevailing model in secondary education in the United States today.

DIFFERENTIATED STAFFING

Differentiated staffing supported by IT resources and e-learning strategies can provide a more effective and efficient model of content delivery. In a differentiated staffing model, different teachers provide different services during the course of the school year. Those who are best at instructional design may plan and develop lessons and courses. Those who are best at presenting the content conduct the lectures, and if the school is really being efficient and inventive these are videotaped, digitized, and stored for access via streaming video anywhere and anytime learners can get access to the Web. Once on the video server, they can be used year after year, and students can review them as many times as they like. Other teachers may design and implement assessments or supervise students who are engaged in e-learning activities. Others may provide face-to-face and online tutorial assistance for students taking the course. Still others may mentor small groups working collaboratively via the Web on authentic learning projects related to the lesson or unit of study.

In differentiated staffing approaches, personnel do jobs of varying skill that require different levels of preparation. This logically suggests differentiated pay scales as well. Both these points present obstacles to the implementation of differentiated staffing in American education. In K–12 education, it is the culture that is most difficult to change, not the technology. Even in the face of blistering criticism across society, public and private schools maintain their culture and practices with little discernable change. However, the dynamics of public education are changing as never before, and we believe that elements of traditional school culture will show signs of fading by 2007. The forces behind the change are varied and not well understood by educators or by the e-learning companies that are developing a presence in the market.

CHANGING DYNAMICS OF K–12 EDUCATION

The growing national teacher shortage will be one catalyst that could bring about change, finally. Fewer people are going into teacher training programs at a time when more and more are required to maintain the traditional school and classroom. The school-aged population continues to grow, and the push for smaller class sizes in an attempt to raise test scores compounds the shortage created by large-scale retirements. As many as one-third of a teaching staff may roll over in any given year because of retirement, career changes, or burnout. In the face of having no one to fill the empty teacher chair, schools may have no choice but to adopt e-learning as a substitute. By 2007, a maturing teacher corps will be leaving the profession in numbers never before seen. As noted above, private e-learning vendors are trying to strategically position themselves to meet this need over the Web or on hosted servers of e-learning resources.

In a school of 1,200 pupils with a class size that averages twenty pupils, one would expect to find a staff of sixty full-time certified teachers. In a differentiated staffing model, the option exists to fill only a portion of the positions with certified staff, say thirty-five of the sixty. The remainder of the positions could be used to "buy" more support staff in the form of paraprofessionals. These noncertified staff could fit one of several categories according to a school's need. They may serve as instructional assistants, say, new hires coming out of teacher preparation programs or even teachers in training during student internships, or they may be retired personnel who only want to work part time. A school may decide that it needs more clerical assistants to help with the production of materials or to help manage communications with parents and students. Other assistants may assume many of the record-keeping tasks teachers are burdened with. The differentiated approach parallels what is used in industry and the military closely. An average of 1,000 hours of preparation goes into each hour of instruction in the U.S. military, for example. K–12 education has never given attention to lesson design, validation, and refinement through the use of feedback that the training profession has used for decades. Thus, the textbook becomes the curriculum, and the instructional approach is reduced to covering the textbook.

In the differentiated staffing approach, the school is paying fewer fully certified teacher salaries and, without spending more money, will be able to hire more assistants at salaries that are from one-half to two-thirds that of a certified teacher. The net result will place more adults in the school to support instructional delivery via the Web and also provide mentoring and tutoring services to students. In a differentiated staffing model, certified teachers, representing the very best at planning and teaching, would be paid higher salaries and would be freed to utilize more of their time to perform duties befitting their professional preparation. All of this could be realized without increasing the cost of providing public education in the district. Indeed, costs could come down as fewer certified teachers are needed to design and produce digital materials over time.

MODELS OF SCHOOL ORGANIZATION

The pyramid in figure 5.1 shows a rough estimate of how a typical school today is staffed in terms of the proportion of expenditure for each category. The U.S. Department of Education estimates that more than 80 percent of all funds go to support individual classroom teachers. They are paid the same regardless of performance, and the relative high cost of populating hundreds of thousands of classrooms with certified, professional teachers robs the school budget and precludes much of anything else. The tiresome task of repeating identical lessons six or more times a day leaves little time for thoughtful planning or creativity, especially when added to other clerical and behavior management tasks that go along with classroom instruction.

The slowness of schools to adopt and use IT suggests, among other things, that it is not practical for school personnel in their current roles to assume new technical tasks, even with extensive or limitless training afforded them. There are ample situations in which this has been tried, and yet teaching staffs still make minimal use of the IT resources provided them. We believe, rather, that a different organizational model that places more adults with different backgrounds into the school setting without raising the total cost of operating the school would overcome the problem of time and motivation of teachers to use IT (see figure 5.2). The mix of adults who would work in such a school would necessarily represent different formal preparation, different skill sets, and different career expectations. Most of the adults in the school would be ad hoc members of the staff. They would complement a small core of what are really master teachers, drawn from the ranks of those currently teaching, who possess the necessary skills and attitudes to be worthy of the title "master teacher." Using the same budget it takes to maintain a traditional organizational

School Organization

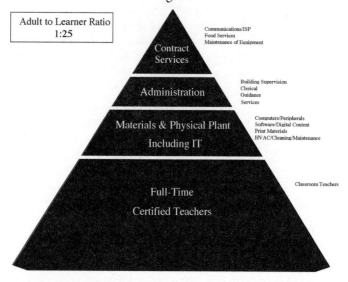

Figure 5.1. Typical Organization of Today's School

School Organization

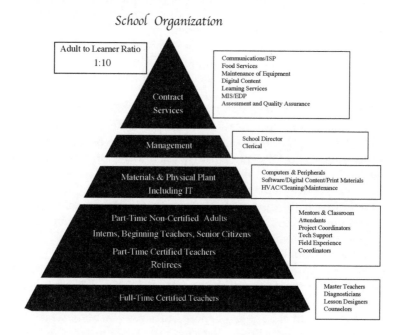

Figure 5.2. Possible School Organization with Differentiated Staffing

model, a school using a differentiated staffing approach could hire more noncertified people with fewer dollars. This would reduce the learner-to-adult ratio. At the same time, the same budget could provide more money to spend on digital resources and pay master teachers a wage befitting their professional skills. The core of master teachers would supervise the other adults who would attend to students in groups and classes as they interacted with digital content, worked on projects, and planned field trips and work experiences. Master teachers would be freed to design and develop learning experiences, counsel individual students, and broker links among learning organizations and learning service providers. The role of the principal and office staff would become less of a top-down administrative task and more geared toward building and managing the different groups and resources the school uses. Another change for teachers and former administrators would be in the relations between them. The new relationship would probably become more like that enjoyed by partners in a law firm than the current employer–employee relationship that exists between principals and teachers.

The professionals on staff would have at least part of their salaries tied to performance, and they would have to collaborate and cooperate to make that part of their salaries. There are today experiments with different organizational models, and these will increase between 2001 and 2007. The real impact of differentiated staffing, however, will come in the midterm future after 2010, when the concept has demonstrated success in a wide range of settings. Communities will have to get used to the new organization in order to transfer their trust and support.

NEW MARKETS FOR MASTER TEACHERS

By 2007, we believe, many of the functions now provided by schools and districts will have begun to be assimilated into fee-based services provided by outside vendors. Well-designed and validated lessons will be available from video server farms. Schools will contract to use these services and so will the home. Schools will pay for services on a per-pupil or per-use basis. Some of the best instructional designers and lecturers will leave K–12 classrooms and go to work for e-learning companies where the pay is better. Their workplaces will most likely be their homes. Therefore, even if schools and districts do not readily adopt differentiated staffing with differentiated pay scales, change can come through the marketplace. We expect such change and feel it will be hastened by teacher shortages. K–12 schools and public school districts will be much more likely to consider differentiated staffing as a solution in the face of escalating costs to maintain the present model. The broad adoption of such a paradigm is not likely to happen by 2007, especially in the public schools. Consequently, the cost of providing K–12 education in the near term will continue to increase until it reaches a break point at which alternatives will have to be found.

DATA MINING AND NEURAL NETWORKS

Standards-based education presents new challenges to K–12 schools that can best be handled with appropriate IT tools and resources. Achieving what amounts to quantum improvements in student performance on higher and higher performance standards will soon take traditional practice to the limits of its capability, and schools, if they survive, will have to adopt practices used by other institutions for many years now. There are techniques that can be said to have produced the tremendous gains in productivity of the American workforce in the last decade of the twentieth century. Simply stated, that workforce has learned to use information to better focus its efforts on increasingly minute levels of detail. At the same time, management has learned more about the changing marketplace by collecting and using information in ways not imagined only a few years ago. Public schools have a simple choice either to adopt and master these techniques or to let other institutions move forward with them and take responsibility of the primary charge to educate the nation's youth. As in all other dimensions of IT that we have examined, public schools face serious obstacles to the adoption of these techniques. Most of these problems are systemic and derive from the culture rather than from finances or the available technology.

For example, public education's critics have repeated loudly and often that the prevailing paradigm of public schooling is designed for mass audiences where curriculum and instruction function like the bed of Procrustes, that is, individuals must use and conform to the lesson as it has been prepared for an entire class. Some learners get it and many do not. Modest remediation efforts may be offered those who do not get it, but such efforts are limited and generally unfocused. As IT has fueled a revolution in personalized services in other fields, so it can enable personalized learning plans for individual students. We believe that by 2007 there will be strong pressure on schools to provide individual learners with customized learning plans to suit their learning styles, cognitive development, and academic readiness, among other things. Doing so will be facilitated by a technology widely used in such fields as nuclear engineering, diesel mechanics, battlefield management, and even stock market investing. The technique relies on the technology of neural networks and has been called data mining.

What is data mining? It is a different process from the way data have traditionally been used, for example, statistical analysis, management reporting, and data display or data visualization. Data mining is a relatively new approach that relies on techniques that were first used to try to teach machines to learn and attempt to mimic the neural networks of the human brain. These techniques are built around algorithms that have their origin in research in artificial intelligence. Data mining does not replace other approaches to the use and analysis of information, but it does supplement them and can provide results they cannot. In one sense, the data-mining process involves the learning of patterns in data. It identifies patterns and then makes predictions that would elude most, if not all, users of conventional tools and techniques. Data-mining tools can be used to generate prediction models that are based on real time data sets and large comprehensive databases that may encompass an entire organization such as a school.

In summary, data mining in education means finding patterns in data that are used to improve institutional or organizational processes. We prefer another term for this process, *knowledge discovery. Knowledge discovery* seems better suited to the education profession, but either term describes a process of discovering patterns in data that are used to inform decisions. These may be management decisions, such as how many teacher aides are needed in a particular school, or, more to the point, they may be decisions about how to enable a particular student to achieve his or her academic potential in relation to a specific lesson, standard, or concept.

Knowledge-discovery techniques require comprehensive collections of raw data that define a process, an event, or a task. An algorithm or inference engine "mines" those data to identify patterns, trends, and conditions that require attention. Often, this is a fully automated process and may not require human intervention at all. In the case of managing a nuclear power plant, for example, the knowledge-discovery system monitors many thousands of variables to quickly identify a condition, a trend, or a pattern that could sooner or later cause problems. An alert is signaled, and, most likely, the system itself will respond by adjusting one or more variables. In some cases, the adjustment may be left to human reaction and judgment. The automated system can monitor more variables and see more patterns, trends, and conditions more rapidly than a human being can. Those industries making effective use of neural networks and knowledge discovery have significant advantages over those that do not. For more information on knowledge discovery, check the on-line magazine *Kdnuggets* at http://www.kdnuggets.com/news.

Knowledge-discovery techniques can be applied to the raw student data that schools routinely collect and store. We believe that as schools learn to use these tools and techniques, they will need and want to collect more complete data sets. The area of metadata (data about data and their sources) has the potential to help teachers and tutors monitor student progress on an hour-by-hour or lesson-to-lesson basis. The use of digital on-line content will enable many categories and types of data to be collected that did not exist prior to the use of digital IT systems. How the cursor is moved or the path a student takes through a learning event can be used to analyze learning style or suggest gaps in prior learning. Systems to monitor learning progress against expected levels of achievement, for example, could quickly alert a master teacher to a problem or to the likelihood that a problem will develop unless some deficiency in the learner's cognitive structure or behavioral pattern is corrected. When minor deficiencies go unnoticed and unattended by teachers, learners develop what we call a "learning debt." Learning debts accumulate over time and can lead to failure, dropout, and lower than expected performance. Reaching one's full potential is significantly facilitated if deficiencies are corrected early and quickly.

Teachers typically report that they know with certainty what their students have learned, what they can do, and what their needs are. In light of the low performance of schools on standards-based assessments today, it is evident that the teachers' knowledge is actually quite shallow or else they do very little with the knowledge if they do have it. Given classes of thirty or more students and total student loads of up to 180 students per day, as is common in traditional secondary schools, no one reasonably expects teachers to have in-depth knowledge of each child's needs in anything other than very general terms. Even reducing class sizes to fifteen or eighteen will not significantly improve a teacher's ability to fully comprehend individual needs. As we capture more and more data at the point where the learning transaction takes place (classroom, home, workplace, etc.), the more potential we create for mining the data to produce accurate profiles for individual learners. The more accurate the profile is, the more likely the learning activity selected for the learner will meet the needs.

The surge in what schools refer to as their special education populations attests to the desire of parents for specialized and personalized services for their children. Parents understand that programs for exceptional education bring more resources to bear on individual needs and that much more thorough programs of assessment are applied to these students to ensure that their needs are met. When public schools are unable to provide the levels of personalized services that parents expect, they will turn to private sources that do offer them. In 2001, Sylvan Learning Systems is beginning to offer these services and openly advertise them on television.

Data mining is practiced very little, if at all, in K–12 education as this volume goes to press. We believe that data mining will be more complex for schools to implement than it has been in business, industry, or military applications. There are so many more variables involved in the teaching and learning process, and, because there are more variables and more sources of data, these elements will tend to be more complex in their interactions with one another.

Data mining or knowledge discovery will be experimented with in a limited fashion by the more technologically advanced schools and districts between 2001 and 2007. Companies like Sylvan will learn from their early efforts and extend their diagnostic services to include individual lesson plans. Beyond 2007, public education will be called on to provide very personalized services that only such techniques as data mining can enable. We will come back to data mining in the chapter that covers the period 2008–14. It is in that time frame that K–12 education will be ready to utilize such tools and techniques.

WHY SCHOOLS WILL INITIALLY ADOPT KNOWLEDGE-DISCOVERY TECHNIQUES

Traditional data-processing and analysis tools provide primarily summative, or after-the-fact, information. The purpose of knowledge-discovery applications is to provide formative information. Formative information functions as immediate feedback so that learning materials, instructional strategies, learning goals and objectives, and support resources can be realigned with the results that have already been produced. The vision for these tools is to create automated systems with a capacity to "watch" individual learner or teacher performance, day to day, and identify areas of need at the moment they arise. It is not without reason to expect tools such as these in their mature form to be able to suggest intervention strategies or solutions. The private sector and government have already demonstrated the viability of such systems, but schools are simply not in a position to utilize them. Their data collections are not organized around their "business side," or classroom, and their IT departments are not used to data-mining strategies and approaches. Too often, IT or management information system departments operate their own networks and servers apart from anything the instructional side of the enterprise does. They provide a few regular reports that offer limited views of limited data sets. If one needs anything else, that could be a problem.

Those districts that begin to use the tools first will define the all-important concept of organizing data processing around the real business and the real product of schools: learning. Early adopters of data-mining techniques will demonstrate that the tools are not "snake oil" and that they can provide new and more comprehensive uses of information that inform decision making right down to the day-to-day business of the classroom. At the same time, early adopters will position themselves to provide essential expert advice to others in terms of the design and set up of systems as well as teaching others what to look for, where to look, and how to follow up on patterns once they are found. Knowledge discovery will provide the formative feedback that will enable the teaching profession to finally align all the elements involved in teaching and learning (curriculum, instructional technique, learning content and support material, support personnel, and the rest of the community).

Some early and attainable goals for knowledge discovery in K–12 education include such things as providing automated predictors of student performance at the end of a course or lesson based on present condition. Another is suggesting intervention procedures to overcome learning debts. Knowledge-discovery techniques could also provide automated predictors of teacher and school performance overall at the end of a course or lesson. These are baby steps, but they represent movement in the right direction.

Those who assume leadership roles in knowledge discovery in K–12 schools will have to be able to help new users make sense of the products of knowledge discovery, especially what indicates less than acceptable performance and what the indicators of failure are. Unfortunately, the IT industry is not in a position now to provide leadership to K–12 education, given its limited experience with the institution and its limited knowledge about human learning.

HOSTED SOLUTIONS, APPLICATION SERVICE PROVIDERS, AND OUTSOURCING

For some schools and districts, the complexity of utilizing IT to anything like its full potential presents obstacles that exceed the capacity of their financial and staff resources. For them, one solution may be to find partners that are willing to share the cost of providing resources and services, or they may simply hire a commercial firm to provide and support part or all of their IT activities. Recently, the Detroit Public School District announced that it would outsource its entire IT enterprise, including, among other things, the purchase and installation of classroom computers and data-processing services. It entered this arrangement with the belief that it will be cheaper in the long run, and the vendor believes that it can deliver a satisfactory level of service and make a profit doing so. The Detroit experiment will be watched closely by others who are considering a similar arrangement. Shortages of qualified personnel to fill district IT positions will likely force some districts to follow a similar path.

By 2007, schools will have to provide more information services to support their instructional efforts; at the same time they will be expected to provide comprehensive IT training and experiences for their students. The pressure from these two centers of need will cause the period between 2001 and 2007 to be characterized by the sudden appearance of new models of providing and supporting IT services for schools and their just as sudden demise. Districts with the capability to do so may well attempt to provide services for less capable districts on a contractual or shared-cost basis. Previously, we have discussed how some districts will develop and provide digital content for the curriculum and perhaps host distributed learning services as a fee-based service for others. Other approaches being floated to schools today include hosted Internet services and application service providers (ASPs).

A hosted service may focus on a district's website or on its student information system. Vendors, individual school districts, regional service centers, and state departments of education, will experiment with the business of hosting services by 2007. In the Hampton Roads area of Virginia, the public television station WHRO hosts services for local public and private schools. This model has been in place for almost twenty years and is deemed successful by the participants. One key to its success has been the relationship the public television station has developed and maintained with the schools and districts. Given direction by a regional planning group called the Consortium for Interactive Instruction (CII), all participants have real ownership of the products and services produced. The consortium membership represents public and private schools, the station itself, NASA's Langley Research Center, and local universities. You can learn more about the CII at http://whro.cii.org.

ASPs have had some success in the private sector and are looking at the public sector as a large viable market. These services allow end users to access fast, powerful servers on the vendor's premises for a wide range of applications including basic productivity software. For example, instead of purchasing thousands of licenses of Microsoft Office, a firm (or school district) may purchase a concurrent user license from an ASP, say 500 concurrent users. Then, up to 500 people at a time would be able to access and use the software residing on the vendor's servers. The vendor manages the licenses, provides the software via the Web, and maintains it. The end user is freed from any and all license fees as well as installation and maintenance tasks.

On the surface at least, the ASP approach looks attractive to firms and schools with limited resources. The device on the user's desk can be much less powerful. Because the processing is taking place on the host server, a cheaper piece of equipment can be used for the client. There remain a number of questions to be answered, however. How scalable can the ASP model be? As schools begin to achieve one-to-one computer-to-student ratios, they are likely to need more than 1,000 concurrent users for basic productivity software, and a school district may have dozens or scores of schools. ASP providers will have difficulty meeting that level of demand. Using the infrastructure of the school to launch and run application software will quickly render it useless for any other activity such as distributed learning, access to research resources on the Web, and so on. The cost of adding additional bandwidth to support ASPs could exceed any savings in licenses and support. There is also a question about how reliable the service can be made to be. Any interruption in communications between the vendor and the school will stop all IT activity. On the other hand, when individual PCs use LAN resources there are built-in redundancy factors in the system. If one machine breaks, there are others that can be used in the meantime. If one leg of the network goes down, others will still be available.

Security presents another major stumbling block for the ASP model. A large server farm presents a much more attractive target for hacker attacks than a school district server and offers a greater potential for catastrophic loss of data. The confidential nature of student data represents still another area of concern. If mighty Microsoft cannot protect its internal servers from intrusion, can the public expect security from vendor services that have been contracted on a low-bid basis? Finally, one has to wonder how willing the end user community will be to give up control of valuable IT tools and resources? The ASP model, in effect, recentralizes the computing experience in ways reminiscent of the days of mainframe computing and "green stamp" resource sharing. (A green stamp in those days equated to a minute of use on the mainframe computer, where demand often exceeded the computational power of the machine. Therefore, resources had to be rationed.) Undoubtedly, many public school customers will simply feel insecure about their mission-critical software and data when they are running on someone else's computer. In spite of these concerns, however, many schools will experiment with ASPs in the coming years.

We do not expect the ASP trend to survive as a major player beyond the near term. The ASP approach seems a step backward to people who are used to full-functioned personal computers and devices that can work with or without a network connection. We have already made the case that the future use of IT in schools will be characterized by multimedia-rich digital content and applications that require increasingly higher levels of processing power and network capacity. Consequently, we believe that local networks and personal computers are more capable than those based on a Webcentric approach, and only limited use of ASPs is likely to survive the near term.

Finally, on the matter of outsourcing in public education, it is one thing for public schools to enter into a partnership with a public, nonprofit institution and quite another for them to partner with for-profit corporations. The close and even structural relationship that WHRO enjoys with school districts through the CII looks very attractive to IT vendors that could provide the same kinds of services, and many of them are attempting to establish such partnerships today. Problems arise in terms of conflict-of-interest concerns by local and state governments that must be careful about how noncompetitively bid services provided by the private sector may be viewed by the public and other vendors. To a degree, the success of IT in the private sector has been supported by close partnerships among corporations, their business customers, and their supply chain. Just-in-time inventory, training, and other services have helped to contain costs and increase productivity. While we expect to see many new kinds of relationships among schools, districts, and IT vendors, the real impact of these on public education will come after 2007 as both the culture and the business processes of schools and local governments undergo change.

FLUENCY IN INFORMATION TECHNOLOGY

Fluency in information technology, or FITness as the National Research Council has called it in its book *Being Fluent with Information Technology*,[1] is rapidly becoming a topic of concern for both educators and the public at large. Fluency as it is defined by the council is much more than what has been implied by the term *computer literacy*. Fluency in IT of citizens is becoming more and more vital to modern societies. As such, the need to include IT in the definition of what constitutes basic literacy has already gathered momentum. The need for all citizens to be able to use IT resources, understand them enough to manage them in a democratic society, and manage the technology's impact on human communities will eventually make IT an accepted subject of study in the academic curriculum of elementary and secondary schools.

Once established in the academic (as opposed to the vocational-technical) curriculum, IT will have achieved both legitimacy and acceptance in the school culture. As such, IT resources will be integrated into the operational budgets of schools and districts instead of being an annual budget item whose case must be pleaded yearly before school boards and local governments. IT will have achieved its place alongside water and electricity as fundamental to the existence of public education. We will see the fluency begin to assume its place in school curriculums by 2007 and become firmly established there by 2014.

SUMMARY

As we near the end of the period we have called the near-term future, some obvious changes will have been realized in public education, many made possible by information technologies. We do not expect to name them all, and of those we will name, none will represent change on a scale to qualify as a paradigm shift. The following list represents some of the technology-enabled changes that we believe will be prevalent in schools by 2007:

- Lesson plans on demand enable a district's teachers to draw on a central server of lesson plans that have been centrally designed. Additionally, teachers will find many similar resources on the Web and modify them to meet district standards.
- Teaching strategies will be available in similar fashion. These, also, may have been locally designed and developed, and many techniques found on the Web will be locally modified by master teachers serving as instructional designers and developers.
- Distance and distributed learning courses on demand will be commonly available on the Web. These courses will serve adult learners but increasingly come to serve a larger portion of the traditional K–12 school population.
- Complete banks of lessons for core academic courses will be available on demand for students who need remedial assistance or for those whose learning pace is faster than what the traditional school is offering on site. Personal mobile computers will enable learners to access the materials from home or other Internet access points in the community (public libraries or museums).
- Individual learning plans for a course, a year, a career goal, or a life goal will be well on their way to universal availability for all learners.
- Year-round schools will be widespread. They are appearing on the landscape in regularity today. Rather than invest heavily in new construction, localities will begin to seek to leverage the resources they have by using them more of the time. Technology will facilitate communications and leverage instructional staff in year-round schools.
- Virtual schools and distributed learning will be in wider use, initially to supplement curriculum in small and rural districts and later as a way to contain the cost of education in larger districts. Labor shortages and the cost of transporting students will also fuel the adoption of virtual school models. Communications technology will have improved such that individuals can be linked with relative ease into ad

hoc learning groups for particular lessons as well as complete courses of study.

- Personal digital devices of one type or another will empower learners. Indeed, such devices will become a necessity as the phenomenon of "digital fusion" continues to replace paper-based learning content with digital content. Each student will have multiple devices, some, if not all, of which will be programmed with resources designed to meet his or her particular needs. They will also contain or link to a portfolio of that student's actual work. The current trend toward mobile devices will have freed most users from the tether of the hard-wired network.

- Public libraries and museums will assume expanded roles and receive increased funding to function as learning resource centers where students can go when school resources or personnel are not available.

- More teachers will have flexible schedules and experience significant changes in their duties and responsibilities. They will be expected to serve as members of resource pools to mentor and tutor individual students.

- Differentiated staffing will be in the early stages of becoming the norm, and the best of the teacher corps will begin to rise to the top and assume the more complex duties of instructional design, development, and assessment.

- The expansion of home schooling will continue but with broader support from public schools, private vendors, museums, and public libraries through the use of the Internet.

- Schools will be expected to be linked to the home and other human resource agencies. Again, the Internet will propel the integration of services, for these groups all serve the same client.

- Knowledge-discovery technology will have begun to enable schools to focus more closely on individual students than on classes and grade levels. Individual education plans for all students will be well on the way to becoming a norm and not an exception. By 2007, we will have seen successful tests of automated systems that not only identify patterns and potential problems but also suggest interventions and remedies. Commercial interests will be more likely to offer these services than K–12 schools will be, however.

- New relationships among schools, other public institutions, and commercial vendors of IT services will be more common. New collaborations between districts and other public service agencies will begin to create broader services for lifelong learning and new kinds of learning institutions that will emerge between 2008 and 2014.

NOTE

1. National Research Council, Committee on Information Technology Literacy, *Being Fluent with Information Technology* (Washington, D.C.: National Academy Press, 1999). Available at http://books.nap.edu/books/030906399X/html/index.html0.

6

The Midterm Future of Technology in Education: 2008–14

By 2008, events in the world outside the schoolhouse combined with continuing evolution of IT will have brought K–12 education to what some are calling the break point. For K–12 schools the break point will be the point at which transformation to a new model will be inevitable. What will it take to reach break point? The combined influence of connectivity to global networks and ubiquitous digital content will render obsolete many of the traditional resources and approaches schools have used for more than a century to foster the intellectual development of learners. The preceding period, what we have called the near-term future, will have been characterized by a wide range of experiments in learning and schooling by both public and private groups. The ability to capture digital information at every transaction point in the learning process will enable assessment and monitoring capabilities that schools have never had to contend with before. Accountability will be tight, and the price of failure, very steep for any learning organization that does not and cannot meet expectations. Successes and failures of schools, programs, teachers, and learning strategies will be revealed instantly by newly implemented knowledge-discovery systems. Schools everywhere, public and private, will be under intense pressure to adapt themselves around the most successful models that will come out of this period. Commercial vendors of learning services will be offering solutions where schools do not or cannot. The period 2008 through 2014 could be an exciting time to be involved in K–12 education, or according to the most severe critics of American education, it may be a time that will mark the end of schools as we know them.

WILL K–12 EDUCATIONAL INSTITUTIONS
SURVIVE THE MIDTERM FUTURE?

Among the strongest critics of public education are those who maintain that we must completely let go of our old "legacy" system in order to build a new one from the ground up. "The new can't be built on top of the old system," they maintain. Whether this is true or not poses one of the biggest questions about public education that will be answered by 2015. As a friend and superintendent in New York once put it, "Can public education find within itself (perhaps with strong support from the private sector and with incentive from state and national governments) the vision and the gumption to make itself relevant?" That is, can a system of public education that was designed for the Agricultural Age and then modified to accommodate the needs of the Industrial Age now change itself enough to adequately serve the Information Age? However the public and private K–12 schools of America respond to the changing world around them, the foundation will be set for a major transformation in how people learn during the period 2008–14. Whether our system of K–12 education will survive the period is not an easy question to answer because our educational enterprise is far more complex and much more embedded into the fabric of our lives than we imagine. More is at stake than technology can address.

Who is the "we" who will make change happen? Will it be the teachers and administrators who have built careers around the existing system of education? If so, society is asking them to work themselves out of the job they love and know how to perform, the job they have been trained to do. What is the motivation for them to tear down what has become a very comfortable system and build something entirely new, something that will likely put all professionals back to square one on the career ladder? Real change comes in response to needs that are strongly felt and when the choice not to change no longer exists. People under pressure search for relief. When the pressure is great enough, alternatives will be found elsewhere if changes cannot be made to the existing system. The "system" has not changed appreciably so far because that point of necessity has not been reached, and, at the same time, satisfactory alternatives are not in place either. Finally, there is an element of truth in the saying that bureaucracies exist primarily to carry on themselves.

LET THE FUTURISTS BEWARE

Today, one will find varied opinions about the continuation of our traditional K–12 school model. The end of K–12 education as we know it has been prophesized often in the last half of the twentieth century, but the institution has sustained itself remarkably intact while others have been turned inside out and upside down by the forces of technology and societal change. Historically, taking the view that our traditional K–12 education system will fade into history has been a dangerous one for futurists to hold. Nevertheless, we believe that a much changed education system capable of serving a twenty-first-century American society will begin to take shape as early as 2008. We further believe that whatever the changes will be, they will be driven by information technologies. IT will influence change directly by providing learners with alternatives to whatever model of K–12 education exists at the time (public and private). IT will also indirectly impact K–12 education through the changes it is bringing to society, changes that alter the expectations citizens have for their institutions.

While the private sector bemoaned the slowness of education to embrace change in the 1990s and early 2000s, it missed the point that changes outside the schoolhouse continue to accumulate and will inevitably reach a critical mass that will make either transformation of schools happen or their extinction unavoidable. Therefore, if K–12 educational institutions of 2001 survive the period ending in 2014, they will be very different places compared with what we have today simply because the world will be very different.

E-LEARNING BECOMES THE NORM

The phenomenon of e-learning began to rise to prominence soon after schools gained access to the Internet. It will be widely experimented with between 2001 and 2007. The number of e-learning ventures will develop exponentially during this period, both within and around K–12 institutions. The dynamics that will continue to drive the shift from traditional classrooms to e-learning venues between 2008 and 2014 are many. Count among them the fact that when and where people want to learn have been changing for more than a decade, a trend clearly marked by rises in home schooling, distributed and distance learning, and the growth of commercial learning companies such as Sylvan Learning Systems and Advantage Learning. The growing need for lifelong learning beyond K–12 education and beyond graduate school will spur demand for anywhere, anytime learning solutions.

By 2014, examples of fixed-place and fixed-time learning will be difficult to find. Since the late twentieth century, it has become increasingly difficult for people, adolescents among them, to take time away from work to attend traditional classes. We first witnessed this as many high school graduates had to work their ways through college. Recently high school–aged students are working in jobs that compete for time with the regular school day. It has become a fact of life in the twenty-first century that people of all ages have more to learn as human knowledge expands. The more we know, the more we have to learn and the more we have to unlearn, a fact that requires more efficient approaches to instructional design and content delivery. Trends in society clearly indicate that people will continue to need to accelerate the rate of learning as time available to dedicate to formal learning decreases from adolescence upward and as the need for lifelong learning becomes more central to success and happiness. It is clear today that learners need to learn more efficiently than the traditional classroom model is allowing them to do.

Oddly, the antithesis is also true. The recognition by cognitive science that some learners require longer to learn than others means that learning systems must provide for review and repetition and make it easier for learners to pace themselves while choosing among multiple learning strategies. Parents and children will select learning services that best accommodate the child's needs. Tutors, multimedia resources, peer support groups, and study groups all require more time and more choice than traditional schools and classrooms have been able or willing to provide. The period 2001–07 will be a prime growing season for new approaches to learning from kindergarten through retirement and beyond, and the period 2008–14 will be the period during which the best of these are consolidated into new approaches to schooling and learning. Many models will be tested by K–12 schools and districts and, especially, by other, nontraditional providers of learning services to the K–12 age group.

Some schools will enter the period 2008–14 more adept at offering individualized services, based on knowledge-discovery applications that help teachers and counselors monitor learner progress and individual interests and needs. Some will not. Whether the best of K–12 schools will be adept enough to keep many of their customers from going to private services is debatable. The rich offerings from media and Internet companies that have ventured into K–12 learning services will attract a sizeable portion of the learning market at the upper income levels particularly. There is real reason to be concerned that, for a while at least, public schools will serve primarily the lower socioeconomic levels while the upper and middle classes move on in search of providers that offer more and better services. What we call the digital divide in 2001 will become a learning divide if such a break occurs. Pressure on governments to provide equal educational access for all may well take away from traditional schools even clients in the lower socioeconomic classes if vouchers or other funding mechanisms that make more of the education dollar available for parental choice are adopted. If schools cannot compete in the competitive diverse learning environment we envision, they may cease to exist in many communities by 2014.

BEYOND VIRTUAL CLASSROOMS

By 2008, learning, wherever it takes place, will involve ubiquitous computing for nearly all learners beyond primary school age. What we now call virtual classrooms will have become ad hoc learning places that come and go in cyberspace in response to the needs of individuals and small groups. Many virtual classrooms will be augmented to one degree or another by face-to-face sessions in schools or other designated learning places such as libraries and museums. There will be many models and many providers of learning services in addition to the public school system and private K–12 schools. Many of these providers are in business today working with and learning to serve K–12 institutions as a market. Many of what are today business-to-school relationships will become business-to-learner relationships by 2008 as e-learning comes of age.

Parents of children and adolescents will begin to use commercially provided services at a more frequent rate throughout this period. Services will include assessment, diagnosis of learning styles and difficulties, and the development of individualized learning programs, highly personalized and tailored for specific learners. It will not be difficult to monitor the percentage of the population that will use these services each year. We need only watch the stock market reports on the e-learning industry to quantify its progress. Individualized learning programs will be expected by parents because they more accurately reflect the readiness levels, learning styles, and life goals of their children than the mass curriculum offered by schools today. Providers of individualized learning plans will complement rather than supplant school-based services in the early stages, but, for those who can afford them, beyond 2010 the alternatives will be much too attractive and too effective for them to ignore. By 2010 commercial e-learning will begin to supplant both public and private school services for a growing segment of the population.

DATA MINING GROWS IN IMPORTANCE

Data-mining techniques that began to come into play in the 2001–07 period will be routinely used by the private learning services sector by 2010. Unfortunately, many schools and districts will not have developed the ability to use data-mining techniques and show little interest in them at the moment. Commercial learning service providers will have been collecting data on learners based on their interactions on the Web with digital content. They will also collect data on interests and natural learning patterns as their clients use the Web for entertainment. If schools do not learn to collect and use data in a similar fashion, they simply will not be able to offer comparable services. Without reliable and comprehensive knowledge about individual learners, personalized education plans are not possible.

CONTENT DELIVERY: NEW CHOICES

We expect that throughout the early years of this period, say, 2008–10, content delivery (presenting learners with content to be learned) will continue to have its locus and control at the school, especially for the youngest learners. Schools, after all, are organized for this purpose above all others. However, as broadband connectivity reaches homes, libraries, and museums, these institutions along with commercial providers will begin to supplant more and more school-based services for content delivery. The supplanting of schools for content delivery will begin in a limited fashion but will increasingly cover a broader range of subjects and grade levels. The rate at which content delivery is subsumed under commercial services will depend in part on the availability of teachers to fill classrooms and broadband access at home and work. Therefore, expect to see broad use of commercial content delivery in the areas of math and science first and expect it to come first to those communities with extensive broadband infrastructures. Rural areas are likely to be losers in this dimension of learning.

Some colleges and universities may emerge with the capability and the goal to extend their full-time equivalent enrollments by reaching into the student population at grades 11 and 12 during this period. Already, many juniors and seniors in high school take courses for college credit. Dual enrollment options (high school seniors and college first-year students) have been available from community colleges for many years. It is not uncommon for able students to leave high school with enough college credit to allow them to finish a baccalaureate program in three years instead of four. Those institutions of higher education that have developed distance and distributed learning capabilities are likely to be winners in this period. Finishing in three instead of four years is one way to reduce the cost of college for parents.

Major corporations are also very likely to enter the e-learning arena in a significant way. Ventures such as Cisco and Oracle Academies are but the beginning for corporate America to influence first curriculum and ultimately the delivery of instruction in ways that will ensure an adequate workforce for the twenty-first century. Each new venture presents learners and their families with choices they have never had before, and once choice becomes an option, it will be impossible to fall back to a model that requires that everyone fit the same mold.

REAL CHOICE: FINALLY

Parents, armed with in-depth and reliable information about their children, and learners themselves will select from numerous providers of learning services specific elements of a learning plan. The range of choices to implement the plan will increase throughout the period 2008–14. Selection may be based on the particular content being offered. Creationism rather than evolution in the science curriculum, for example, may appeal to a particular group of parents. On the other hand, the choice may be based on the instructional approach that the provider uses. Undoubtedly, many choices will be based on the location of the service as well as the time or times it is available. Implementation of a learning plan for any given learner will probably involve multiple providers. The public school system may or may not participate in the delivery or implementation of particular students' learning plans depending on the choices of parents and learners. By 2014, the ability of a particular school system or school to compete in the market for individualized services will determine its relative value and place in its community. Some will have limited scope and influence, while others will become the default choice of parents for the complete range of learning services. Those K–12 schools and districts that retain their primary positions in K–12 learning in their communities will likely be those that have been busy for many years building capacity and infrastructure—all along with an eye to hosting services for traditional students while reaching out to new constituencies. Possible new clients for K–12 schools and districts may include other school districts, parochial and private schools, and the schools of other nations. The most creative of schools and districts will have developed partnerships with business and industry and will be in a position to offer e-learning services to their employees to meet their need for lifelong learning.

VENTURE CAPITALISTS AND K–12 EDUCATION

Initially, those families that can most easily afford commercial services will take advantage of them. Many do so now, as evidenced by a significant increase in home schooling and increased demand for on-line and other commercial learning services and materials. Venture capitalists are just beginning to recognize the investment potential of companies that have successfully positioned themselves for what promises to be a growing and lucrative market that will expand dramatically beyond 2008. Venture capitalists tend to be conservative in their approach to the K–12 education market given the institution's ability to retain its monopoly on access to public funds for education. Neither vouchers nor significant levels of public funding for alternative approaches have materialized to date. Though the total K–12 education budget exceeded $330 billion in 1999, it is estimated that less than $25 billion was available to be spent in the private sector (the bulk of K–12 school funding today is eaten up by personnel costs, up to 80 percent of all education funds, according to the U.S. Department of Education). Added to the problem of limited funds is the difficulty of doing business with an institution as bureaucratic as K–12 education. Both factors make private sector expenditures on learning services more attractive. Hence, we see a shift in emphasis by the IT industry from the business-to-school model to a business-to-customer model that will be especially active between 2008–14. Out of this shift will come many alternatives for parents of children in K–12 education that have not existed before. The shift will also create many new career options for the best and brightest teachers, who will be drawn to better working conditions and higher salaries.

One way to monitor the penetration of commercial services into the overall K–12 learning market will be to note changes in the expenditures in key areas. For example, the home market expenditure for education-related products of all kinds was estimated to be $2.1 billion in 1999, according to the U.S. Department of Education. In terms of tutoring and diagnostic services, it is estimated by private industry sources that this market was at $1.5 billion in 1999 and growing at a rate of 24 percent per year.[1] By monitoring growth in expenditures over time, the degree of movement of learning services from public to private providers can be reliably monitored.

THE END OF TEXTBOOKS

By 2014 we will have reached the end of the print era for most learning content. Digital content will have become the predominant medium for learning resources. Print materials will be the exception. Several obstacles that have prevented wide adoption of digital content will have been overcome in the process. The absence of format standards will be the first to fall. Established by 2008, standards for content will allow access to digital resources via a variety of small, mobile, interactive devices. The emergence of standards will be accompanied by improved compression algorithms that will significantly enhance the storage capacities of small devices such as eBooks. The ability to store more information will effectively allow inexpensive, portable devices to handle multimedia content as effortlessly as present-day devices handle text.

Equally significant, the question about who owns content will be settled toward the middle of this period as copyright legislation and new and easily understandable definitions of fair use policies are established. To fully understand the power of digital content accessed electronically on-line, one has to recognize that much of what is copyrighted learning content in today's textbooks is little more than repurposed knowledge that is actually in the public domain in the form of primary resources. As such, projects to repurpose learning content and human knowledge with public funds will make digital resources more available at little or no cost beyond what it takes for on-line access. There are precedents for such projects, such as ongoing federal efforts to preserve and improve access to our visual history and our national knowledge base. An outstanding example is the National Digital Library Program. One of the products to come out of this project provides remote public access to unique collections of Americana that are held by the Library of Congress through a resource that has been years in development. It is called American Memory (see http://memory.loc.gov/ammem). During the 1990s, the American Memory project digitized materials from a wide variety of original sources. These include media such as pictures, text, audiotapes, videotapes, maps, atlases, diaries, letters, speeches, various government records and reports, and even sheet music. The Digital Classroom, a project of the National Archives and Records Administration, is another ongoing effort to bring primary digital resources out of government files, museums, and departments so that learners can access them. Its Web address is http://merrimack.nara.gov/education/. There are many private and state and local government activities as well.

The National Science Foundation is the sponsor of the Digital Library Project. According to its website, the program "manages the Digital Libraries Initiative, a multi-agency (federal) research program to create large knowledge bases, the technology needed to access them, and the means for improving their usability in a wide range of contexts" (http://www.dli2.nsf.gov/). The digital library that is evolving from this project creates a network of learning environments and resources to support science, math, engineering, and technology education. The goal is that the digital library will ultimately meet the needs of students and teachers at all levels, including K–12 education, and will be available in both individual and collaborative settings. Such materials will first supplement but eventually supplant most print-based materials in use today.

In the vision of the National Science Foundation, the project will venture beyond providing traditional library functions such as retrieval of information or archiving of materials. The vision is that it will also enable users to build or access collaborative work areas in cyberspace where they can experience hands-on laboratory activities or use tools provided there for analysis and visualization of the data. Access to remote instruments, probes, and large databases will be included as well as other new capabilities and information resources as they emerge. Expect to find remote platforms for instruments such a telescopes, other scientific instruments, and human explorers in the ocean depths, in earth orbit, and in the far corners of earth and neighboring planets. One example is sponsored by the North Carolina Department of Cultural Resources, which maintains a website at http://www.ah.dcr.state.nc.us/gar that is devoted completely to the ongoing research around the deep-sea wreckage of Blackbeard's ship, the *Queen Anne's Revenge*. From time to time this site produces live video as divers and archaeologists work on the site. Sites such as this exist all over the Web today and will continue to extend the reach of our eyes and minds. Anyone who does not expect the International Space Station to begin to produce digital learning content for K–12 education has missed much of the rationale behind why we are there in the first place, and they have also failed to note the efforts that NASA and the U.S. Department of Energy have been making for more than a decade. Under the Clinton administration, these agencies were given educational missions as well as their traditional missions in energy and space. To learn more, visit the NASA site at http://education.nasa.gov/.

Textbooks can hardly compete with primary resources integrated into a rich multimedia context and available on-line. Even if publishers provide interactive activities and on-line multimedia supplements to their texts or bundle a variety of analysis tools with them, rising high costs for textbooks and printed materials will prevent many schools and learners from choosing them. On the other hand, pricing structures for commercially provided digital content are now at the outer limits of what schools can afford.

We believe that this situation will not last long. Even today, high prices for digital content are causing some schools and districts to create their own digital materials. Students should play a central role in the creation of their learning materials, as they no doubt will do, given the variety found on the Internet today. It is our sincere belief that by 2014, few printed textbooks, if any, will remain in K–12 education beyond grade 4. Highly capable schools and districts will be in the business of creating digital content along with other individuals and commercial ventures.

It is impossible to offer even a fully descriptive list of free digital resources available in 2001. Some of the more notable to consider as primary sources of information are as follows:

- The Russian Digital Libraries Project (http://www.iis.re/RDLP)
- The Memory of the World Project of UNESCO (http://www.unesco.org/webworld/memory/mempage.htm)
- Digital Libraries Initiative (http://www.di2.nsf.gov)
- eLib: The Electronic Libraries Programme (http://www.ukoln.ac.uk/services/elib)
- The Library of Congress Digital Collections and Programs (http://www.loc.gov/rr/digital.html)
- Bibliotheca Universalis (http://www.bl.uk/gabriel/bibliotheca-universalis/index.htm)
- Digital Library Network (http://www.dl.ulis.ac.ip/DLW)

SCHOOLS DIVERSIFY

By 2014, K–12 schools will be characterized by a much more diverse group of professionals and support staff than they have today. Differentiated staffing will be the norm as schools attempt to improve and diversify the services they offer. Efforts by school districts to offer more choice to parents and students through magnet schools, specialty centers, special programs, and on-line services are but the beginning of the shift to personalized services that will require more differentiated staffs. Shifts in the way schools staff are coming about through parental and student demand and will be exacerbated by teacher shortages that will continue throughout this period. Further, the rising cost of maintaining our current model of schooling will have forced deep structural changes in the way schools conduct business. Distributed learning will be a part of every learner's scholastic experience by the end of the secondary school experience. By 2015, the majority of the learner's interaction with his or her learning service provider will be on-line rather than face-to-face.

REINVENTING THE TEACHER

By 2010, the idea that one needs a resident "in-house" expert on physics called a physics teacher to teach physics will be abandoned. In the broadband world of 2010, the best and the brightest physicists in the world may be available to teach physics to any who want to learn it. Subject matter experts will routinely design, develop, and make available for digital archives lessons in their areas of expertise. They will be motivated to do this in the spirit of public service, perhaps rewarded by their employers. Others will do so for profit. Some materials will be marketed to schools and commercial services, and others will be "sold" directly to learners. Anyone with the will, a website, and marketable expertise to share can become a "teacher" and earn revenue from his or her intellectual property, just as textbook authors do today. Master teachers can develop their own repertoires of digital lessons that earn royalties each time they are used. Some will choose to deliver their materials directly to learners via the Internet or its successor, while others will have agents to market their materials to companies that will in turn provide comprehensive databases of digital content to learning service providers.

Many who now call themselves teachers will have become floating facilitators in schools. Their role will be to monitor and support a wide range of authentic learning activities. Another significant part of their work will require them to be available on-line as students in workgroups convene to plan, discuss, and complete activities and assignments. Threaded discussion groups, chat rooms, and listservs are but a few of the kinds of on-line activities that will need to be both monitored and facilitated. The floating facilitator role is likely to take these individuals into the field with students as often as it places them in self-contained classrooms.

MASTER TEACHER CORPS

By 2010, the profession will begin to be characterized by a growing corps of master teachers. These individuals will emerge from the pool of technology-skilled teachers who have hard data to show that they are effective. Those who earn the title of master teacher will hold higher paying positions than their less motivated or less capable peers, who will play more limited roles in the schools of the period. Master teachers will devote most of their time to instructional design, work that will include building authentic learning activities and developing digital content to support them. Other master teachers will provide mentoring and tutoring services as they work with individuals and groups of varying size and with special needs. Some master teachers are likely to be part-time employees who have "retired" but are highly skilled and motivated individuals with a desire to continue to work in education in limited and more specialized roles.

Throughout the period of 2001–07 the nation will witness the emergence of a corps of recently retired teachers who will possess IT skills and have the capability to market themselves. They will begin to reenter the profession in specialized roles. In the period 2008–14 this core of entrepreneurial teachers will become a major resource for public and private learning organizations. Schools and districts that want their services will have to bid for them along with the many private ventures providing learning services. These individuals are likely to be most attracted to opportunities to meet their students on-line in cyberspace, without the hazardous drive to school each day.

HYBRID LEARNING ENVIRONMENTS
AND INSTITUTIONAL FUSION

As we have pointed out before, the role a school will come to play in its particular community will depend on many factors. Some schools and districts will be able to provide more services than others. Some may provide relatively few services to learners beyond grade 4 or 5. In cases in which schools are less able to meet the demands for personalized and higher levels of services, they are likely to turn to partners for help. The result will be what we call the hybrid learning environment. We have arrangements between schools and other institutions today that qualify them as hybrids. The creation of hybrid learning environments will gather momentum as bandwidth to the home increases and as we see more powerful computers become tied to more functional software.

Hybrid learning environments are taking shape today as institutions of learning begin to collaborate with one another. This is a process that we call institutional fusion. The fusion process may involve any mix of digital libraries, government agencies, colleges and universities, private laboratories and companies, vendors, and museums, as well as public and private K–12 schools. Artists, publishers, scientists, or anyone with something to offer and the desire and means to do so can and will be linked electronically to one another and to the learners themselves. Some schools may function primarily to validate the sources or providers of learning services and to create links among them. Hybrid learning environments will be much more information intensive and become widely available to students of all ages and needs.

CHANGING MISSION FOR PUBLIC EDUCATION

K–12 schooling as we know it will see its mission undergo significant change by the end of this period. First, the institution that has traditionally served children and adolescents will be serving a broader base of constituents than it does today. The continuing need for lifelong learning and the demands of the workplace are beginning to strain community colleges and others that traditionally provide adult education services. Finding new constituents may be the way that some schools and districts manage to stay in business as their traditional clients move to other providers. The societal need for lifelong learning will mean that schools can no longer lock up very expensive infrastructures and resources at the end of the school day and school year. To earn a justifiable return on investment, others will need to use the resources at the same time that schools have become year round. Schools will run classes into the evening hours and on weekends. With changing missions and different roles to play, by 2010 schools will be adapting to challenges from local employers and the general public to become available around the clock and throughout the year.

CUTTING LOOSE JUNIORS AND SENIORS

The dynamics of the workplace, we believe, will begin to cause some districts to compress their curriculum from fourteen years (Pre-K–12) to twelve years (Pre-K–10). What has been grades 11 and 12 will move to community colleges, corporate settings, or ad hoc virtual learning enterprises better able to accommodate anywhere, anytime learning. Some European schools have been following such a model for some time. This will happen as society needs to provide better services for very young children of working parents. Schools in some communities already accept four year olds. Moving that downward to age three is likely in the midterm future.

Communities beyond 2008 will have more capable and more efficient ways to deal with more common areas of cognitive development or academic learning. Cognitive development beyond the early years of schooling is likely to cease to be the primary responsibility of the school system beyond 2014. However, the development of human individuals involves more than the intellect and cognitive structure, and it may be in these other areas, the affective and the psychomotor domains, that schools may find other new roles to fill. Just as the computer and IT can do some things better, so there are areas of human development best left to face-to-face interactions.

DIMENSIONS OF LEARNER DEVELOPMENT

The fear that in the future children will be staying home taking courses on computers with very little real, live contact with other people is unfounded. While IT facilitates cognitive learning very well, and many new opportunities for cognitive development and content learning will be provided outside school, schools as communities of learners may well assume more direct responsibility for the emotional and affective development of children, an area of human development in which computers will have little to contribute beyond linking people together. We believe that by 2010 schools will spend as much of their human capital trying to impact affective areas of human development as they now do on cognitive development. As the population grows and as advances in communication technology continue to shrink the distances among people, so will the need to communicate and to be able to deal with "people" problems increase the need for adult role models and structured environments to support social and emotional development.

Schools and teachers will be free to begin to focus more of their time and energies on the affective dimensions of development. One possible scenario may see learners come together periodically for face-to-face discussion or to receive specialized tutoring services or career counseling. Perhaps it will be the schools that will manage "real" field trips to places that virtual field trips cannot serve well and use these opportunities to facilitate social and emotional development. Teachers will become less isolated and will have more opportunities to share ideas with their peers. Differentiated staffing between 2008 and 2014 will open the doors for many adults, who before could not meet certification requirements, to play a role in the process of schooling. Senior citizens serving as part-time employees will constitute a significant part of the adult complement of the schools of 2010, whether they worked as teachers before retirement or not. Social skills, organizational skills, and planning skills along with communication abilities will be primary requirements for working with young people in the affective domain.

ARTS AND ATHLETICS

Just as the affective areas of human development may be better served by nontechnology strategies, so may creative and athletic endeavors. Participation in team sports teaches the value of cooperation and goal setting. Artistic productions onstage and in musical groups are also likely to become more central to the schools of 2015. More efficient methods of content delivery and cognitive development will leave more time for these endeavors. Both art and athletics promote authentic learning. Planning, rehearsal, and even production of the play, musical composition, and so on all provide high levels of language experience. Schools working with affective and psychomotor development will not be the silent places classrooms are today. More purposeful language experience is likely to improve the general intellectual development of learners. Studies in psycholinguistics support this, but schools have not incorporated such knowledge into practice. The impact of technology may be to facilitate the use of language rather than silence it, as some have feared.

LEARNERS AS "PROSUMERS"

By 2010, schools will begin to think of their students as customers who are effectively in control of how they learn, just as e-commerce customers are in control of what and where they buy. To use Alvin Toffler's term, learners are becoming *prosumers* of educational services, and beyond grade 6, they are likely to be directly involved in the design of their own individual education plans and how they are delivered.

It is clear, even today, that the roles of students and teachers are changing as Internet-based curriculum becomes more available. At the same time, there is a growing opportunity for the best and the brightest teachers to play a more important role in the lives of students if they are willing to accept the inevitability of an electronically interconnected world as the engine of a new economy and a new society. Those educators who can appreciate that students as customers will have great power to determine how and where they will learn will enjoy the most success because they will be the first to be acclimated to the new order. Those who do not develop skills to work in this kind of world will have little or no role in schools beyond 2014.

TECHNOLOGY: WILL IT BE THERE WHEN WE NEED IT?

Technology itself has to get more powerful, become easier to use, and be much more reliable before it can enable the kinds of learning communities we have presented here. We have every expectation that these features will characterize IT resources and services by 2014. The keys to achieve such goals are known and have already been discussed. The very nature of technological evolution in capitalist systems guarantees success. If something does not meet a need or is not reliable, people will not buy it, use it, or come to depend on it. IT successes built around the continuing refinement of standards will combine with the arrival of broadband infrastructures, growing collections of digital content, and capabilities for data integration and data exchange to have us well on the way to achieving these goals. A new generation of IT resources and tools will have begun to create systems that will all but disappear from the user's consciousness. As a result, the technicalities of IT will concern us very little by 2015. Interactive devices themselves are in the process of being incorporated into appliances for communication and information retrieval that bear little resemblance to the desktop computer we know today.

Pocket computers and other handheld devices are common in 2001, but even more remarkable transformations are in development for the next generation of information tools. For example, IBM has recently unveiled a wearable personal computer that was developed by IBM Japan's Yamato Laboratory. Presently, this is only a prototype, but the concept behind it completely transforms the notion of what a computer looks like and how it is used. The main unit of the device is about the same size and weight as a portable CD player. It utilizes a headset and a miniature hand controller. The prototype is small enough to be worn on the body, and it has all the functionality of a notebook computer. The main unit is connected to a hand controller and a headset with cables, but later products will utilize wireless connectivity. The IBM prototype uses a 233-MHz processor and an IBM microdrive and battery pack. It is only a small step to integrate "heads-up" displays now used in military fighter aircraft that are worn like glasses. Another approach taken by the Xybernaut Company is to attach the computing device to an LCD eyepiece that projects a virtual monitor to the user's eye. For more information on the Xybernaut system and the range of options available for it, see the company's website at http://www. xybernaut.com. Combine such devices with wireless Internet connectivity, and we have a completely new paradigm for IT. It is not unreasonable to envision a time before 2010 when we can put on or otherwise assimilate such devices when a child is born—devices with functionality we cannot envision now. As digital assistants, these devices could monitor our activities and remember the patterns of our behavior that reveal our interests: our dislikes, needs, and wants. Armed with that information, they may even be able to offer guidance or suggestions throughout our lives, getting better as we and they get older.

At this level of its evolution, the IT devices and the techniques that drive them begin to assume capabilities to change what it means to be human. Just as prosthetic devices replace aging and damaged limbs and organs, specialized information-processing devices may be assimilated or attached to human tissue. Such notions are not limited to science fiction at all, and many of the technologies to accomplish them already exist.

TECHNOLOGY: WILL ACCESS BE EQUITABLE?

To answer the question, Will the technology have the capabilities to make the educational future we envision possible? we answer with a very loud yes. On the other hand, disparity of access to technology tools and information resources among regions of the nation are likely to be severe early in the period 2008–14. However, as the nation recognizes the cost of allowing the digital divide to continue to widen, state and federal governments will add infrastructure, tools, and resources to the requirements for accreditation of schools and adjust funding formulas to provide what is necessary. Different states and regions will embrace these programs at different rates. Those with the most to gain by fuller participation in the global, knowledge-based economy are likely to raise the loudest voices for such investment. Being without access has already relegated some communities and their citizens into the social and cultural backwaters of society.

The definition of *equity* will undergo change during this period. Combined with comparisons of the amount spent per pupil will be comparisons of access to basic IT tools and resources in the school and in the home. As K–12 education moves beyond the school walls, equity will have to focus on the total equity of access rather than per-pupil expenditures for school-based experiences. This will mean that learners in communities without equitable access will receive higher percentages of the tax dollar than those where greater access already exists. Per-learner expenditures in such communities of need will probably be higher, even within the same school district, as inequities are discovered. We do not believe that the confidence we express in the nation to meet this challenge is a Pollyannaish one. The election campaign of 2000 saw both political parties placing education at the top of their platforms. Few communities, today, fail to understand the need for infrastructure and access to high-quality learning services if they are to thrive in the Information Age.

By 2008–14 most young adults who are among the one million each year who drop out of school will begin to seek alternative ways to achieve the educational tickets they need to get ahead in the world of work. Some will take advantage of the growing numbers of alternatives offered by the K–12 educational system, while others will choose commercial vendors. Among the younger members of the dropout group will be those who regularly attend school part-time and work twenty or more hours per week in internships or in the service sector. An interesting statistic to monitor if it is available during this period might be called the "drop-in" rate—the percentage of dropouts who return to finish basic schooling in venues other than schools.

It will be increasingly common for school-aged, apprentice IT workers to use their job experiences to augment their high school diplomas to leverage good entry-level positions, all without going to college. A college education for a growing percentage of people will be acquired piecemeal as part of a lifelong learning agenda. Already, in 2001, the college diploma no longer is a guarantee of success in the world of work. What one knows and can do based on skills and abilities gathered from experience frequently carry more importance. The very low demand for liberal arts college graduates in the 1990s when many IT jobs were going unfilled is a clear indicator of the shift. In 2001, what is the market for a history major with no IT skills?

INTEGRATION OF VOCATIONAL AND ACADEMIC EDUCATION

If present trends continue as we expect, as few as 17 percent of new jobs each year will require a college diploma of any kind, but more than 90 percent will require skills and abilities to use IT resources and tools. This trend will gradually lead to the complete integration of what are now vocational-technology schools and academic education. In 2001, the two compete for students as "Vo-Tech" competes for legitimacy. The growing reliance of technical systems on core disciplines (logic, language, math, science) will blur the lines between them. Vocational education is likely to be assimilated into the academic curriculum, as suggested by the trend for computer science high school courses to be developed within the mathematics curriculum instead of the business education curriculum.

NOTE

1. Jefferies and Company, Inc., Equity Research, *e-Learning Industry Report* (May 2000), 24.

7

The Long-Term Future
of Technology in
Education: 2015–21

If the rate of change inside an institution is less than the rate of change outside, the end is in sight.

—Jack Welch, CEO, General Electric

As America enters what promises to be a period of history that will see many new and powerful learning technologies introduced, the question that has come up throughout this book will continue to be asked: Will school as a concept and as a learning place endure long enough to welcome learners through its doors in 2021? The fact that we continue to revisit the question here indicates that we believe that schools will survive the period 2008–14, even if they may have lost some of their responsibilities and quite a few of their students to alternative learning services. By 2015, there will be another important question high school–aged learners will have to face along the issue of what kind of learning service to utilize: Does the world they have inherited afford them a time in their lives when formalized learning remains the primary aim? In 2001 adolescents are reporting to full-time and part-time jobs in record numbers, challenging the priority of school-based learning during adolescence. Many indicators, when taken alone, seem to indicate that both schools and childhood are in jeopardy in the future.

Considering the power of the new learning technologies that will materialize during this period, it is easy to hasten to the conclusion that schools will have little chance of continuing. Given the explosion of human knowledge, it would also be easy to assume that there will be so much to learn that adolescence as we have known it will disappear. However, the future is seldom what it is supposed to be, and there is far more involved in both technology and learning than how IT will evolve and be utilized.

In the preceding chapters we have enumerated many challenges facing K–12 education and examined some of the problems that impede the full use of IT. This has not been intended to signal the inevitable end of K–12 institutions or of childhood. Rather, the intent has been to offer evidence from trends in business, industry, and across society of emerging, new opportunities for K–12 education to redefine itself and new choices that are becoming available to learners. We have also sought to point out some of the pressures that are and will be brought to bear on educational institutions to ensure that they do change. Since the beginning of civilization, societies have provided ways and means for children to come into adulthood equipped to be functional citizens. We believe that both childhood and the schoolhouse will survive the period 2008–14 but that both will be very different at the end of the period compared with how they will be at the beginning.

America and the world will begin the period 2015–21 with technological capabilities that are hard to imagine today, a mere decade and a half earlier. The continued evolution of the processing power of the integrated circuit combined with global standards for data collection and data exchange will enable human beings to have high levels of control over how, where, and when they learn. Through knowledge-discovery techniques people will know much more about themselves and about their children than they do today. They may possess profiles of the intellectual and behavioral potentialities of their children even before they are born. We have not discussed the impact of advances in genetic science and the mapping of the human genetic structure in this volume, but, within fifteen years, genetic data combined with data that will be collected as we live our day-to-day lives will enable us to define a child's intellectual potential in detail. These data can be utilized to make it more likely that every person will achieve his or her full potential.

The ever spreading web of connections among institutions and people will offer what will seem to be limitless opportunities to learn and grow. As we have shown previously, the ability to monitor learning progress on a day-to-day basis is advancing steadily. We believe that by 2021, Americans will not be worrying about the digital divide. By this time all Americans will have access to the web of human knowledge, and they will be able to select from among many personalized learning services that will enable them to realize their dreams and fulfill their potential, enhanced by technological prosthetics for body and mind. This does not mean that we will suddenly find ourselves in an educational utopia but, rather, a world that affords more choices and more opportunities to learn. In place of the debate over the digital divide, the United States will be focused on the educational divide and how its system of school-ing can provide the less fortunate with opportunities to receive the full benefit of these services. Within this debate lies the greatest opportunity for the institution we call school to redefine itself. In addition to the old problems of adolescence, parents will worry that their children are not getting enough exposure to the physical world as they spend more and more time interacting with screens or with artificial "worlds" offered in the name of edutainment or just entertainment. Schools could become places that offer, instead of access to technology, a haven from it—a place to experience a little bit of the physical, analog world.

IT-FREE ZONES AND PLACES

Just as students in the 1990s and early 2000s sometimes found themselves obsessed with what were called Multi-User Domains or MUDs, so may students of 2015 be addicted to much more appealing artificial realities. MUDs are created on-line by individuals who assume identities and play roles that evolve from interaction with one another. The early varieties were no more than group narratives conducted over the Internet. Partici-pants create, within the rules of the domain they are a part of, text-based descriptions of settings and characters. Here, in these imaginary places, they meet, interact, go to battle, and develop long-term personal relation-ships. MUDs started with college students, but in 2001 they involve high school– and even middle school–aged children. MUDs are fantasy worlds with all the allure such places offer. When rich visual details are added to MUDs (as the technology found in the Sony Playstation II is already able to create), the appeal and addictive nature of these virtual experiences will cause parents to worry that the virtual lives of their children have be-come too important and are a detriment to their real world selves and ac-tivities. So school may continue, at least in part, to isolate learners from certain kinds of digital experiences.

SCHOOLS JUST DO NOT GET IT

The quotation by Chairman Welch that begins this chapter will suggest to some that K–12 education is doomed and that we may as well get on with building a new institution. That attitude ignores the oftentimes loud na-tional debate at all levels of government that has been going on for years about how to remake our educational institutions. The debate has been and will become even more intense and focused with the passage of time. Throughout the last two decades of the twentieth century, eager to see real change happen, education's critics have exhibited little patience for an institution that cannot see the "obvious" and react accordingly. The critics fail to realize the complexity and difficulty of making structural change happen within such an institution as "fractured" as U.S. education. K–12 education is not one monolithic organization but, instead, a system of thousands of local communities trying to find the best opportunities for their children and their own lifelong learning needs. In 2001, there is no national consensus about what K–12 education should become even if there existed a great national will to suddenly go and start rebuilding it. Transformation in K–12 education will come one school, one district, and one community at a time, with momentum gathering each passing year, until we find, finally, that we have arrived at a system the meets the needs of the twenty-first century.

In 2001, in spite of the remarkable advances in IT tools and applications that we now possess, those with the potential to actually remake K–12 education are still in the incubator. As we have discussed in the previous chapter, many "flash" trends come into play each year, but only a few survive the pressure of continuous technological innovation or society's willingness to adopt them into the structure of its educational system. With each passing year, K–12 schools and the communities they serve will see with a little more clarity what the real opportunities are. These will be adopted first in one place and then in many. Along the way the majority of the "flashes" will be abandoned, and new ones will take their place and be tested in time. A pattern of IT-based change for K–12 education has already become well established, as witnessed by the way communities have recognized the importance of the computer and invested in them for classroom use. The national effort to wire every school in America that should be complete by 2005 is another example. Many billions of dollars have been invested, and many more need to follow so that refinements can be made and new infrastructures and strategies can be added to the mix as the system continues to build its capacity, for example, wireless technology. The investment has been just enough to test the water of what IT could make out of K–12 education but not enough to enable the change to happen. It is the absence of an adequate investment that reveals the public's ambivalence about giving up, once and for all, the institution of school as we have known it.

APPROACH/AVOIDANCE BEHAVIOR

It is the conservative nature of K–12 schooling that protects it from radical changes that could hurt the very individuals it is supposed to serve. When the time comes that the old simply cannot stand in the face of the new, the old will be abandoned. It always has been. A transformed system of education will emerge. About that there can be no doubt. We believe that the new system will be largely in place as we near the end of the period 2015–21, and its chief characteristic will be a high level of flexibility that will enable the system to accommodate continuous change in structure and processes. Change is the beast technology has wrought, and flexibility of mind and organization has been the way humankind has coped with it. Along the way, communities will face setbacks as they have to redo much of what they attempted in the first two decades of the twenty-first century. If that means building new institutions to accommodate the kinds of programs needed at the time, that is what will happen. Some individuals will suffer personal and professional setbacks if the services they are prepared to offer are no longer needed. In the final analysis, K–12 schoolchildren will learn what they need to learn, and they will do so with more support in the form of better and more efficient services to help them.

CHILDREN OF A NEW AGE

With that said, how will K–12 education be different in 2015? The biggest and most assured difference will lie in the children themselves. Children of 2015 will be very different from the children of 2001, just as children who began school in 2001 were different from their 1990 predecessors. Children entering school in fall 2001 have never known a time when computers and networks were not a driving force in their world. Similarly, children of 2105 will never have known a time when broadband-accessed interactive media were not a force in their lives. They can be dubbed "digital" children, and they will live every day in a society awash with changing technologies. By the time they come to school, at age three or four, they will know something about how to take advantage of new technologies as they emerge. They will be used to choice in all aspects of their lives. Even if schools try, they will not be able to make these children fit or accept a model of education that offers only mass curriculum and instruction. The children will not respond to it, and neither will their parents, who themselves grew up in the digital age in its formative stages. They will not have to accept it. Alternatives will be everywhere, and by 2015 the funding will follow the learner, not flow automatically to the local K–12 school system.

   Children of 2015 will very early develop an intuitive sense that knowledge has a shelf life and that unlearning is just as important as learning. This is another way of saying that they will appreciate the necessity of learning how to learn. By the time they reach high school age, learners of this period will be well aware of the importance of education to their futures. It has long been demonstrated that education levels worldwide are increasing at faster and faster rates. To maintain an edge in a global society, only the best education will do. Armed with this insight and fueled by ambition uncommon in the average high school student of 2001, the learner of 2015 will become an educational activist on his or her own behalf. The trend was evident as early as 2000, when some of the brightest learners had already become prosumers of the services schools offered and had learned to develop alternatives among a growing list of electronic resources, school sanctioned and school provided or not. They also began starting their own companies and seeking internships with high-tech and software firms. The learners of 2015 will also be used to instant gratification and a media-rich environment, and they will tune out and reject experiences that do not offer the same. Therefore, the biggest catalyst for change in this period will be the learners themselves.

In spite of their differences and the new technologies available to them, children of the digital age will still have to learn to read critically, write with impact, listen purposefully, and speak fluently. We do not subscribe to the belief of some futurists that reading and writing will soon be obsolete skills. Even if voice input and voice recognition work flawlessly, efficiency will demand a very high level of skills in reading and writing. Many can read (some can even write) faster than they can listen. Listening, unless we change the nature of language itself, compress it somehow, is just not as efficient as reading, and listening will not supplant reading regardless of powerful technological inventiveness to support advances in speech recognition and speech synthesis.

Like their predecessors since 2000, children of 2015 must be highly skilled when it comes to finding information and understanding it and be able to evaluate its accuracy and reliability. Even more than their predecessors, they must learn how to apply it to personal concerns and opportunities. Their communication skills will be critical to their success both as student learners and as citizens. To a degree that adults who came of age in an analog age can hardly appreciate, learners will have to make the educational system understand who they are and what they seek to become. Their ability to effectively communicate their ideas to diverse groups in different settings will be paramount. They simply cannot and will not sit back and wait for education to come to them. Likewise, their success throughout life will depend more than ever on an ability to understand the ideas and needs of others and to see how their lives can and must blend with those of others to solve problems and create new opportunities.

With the trend of increased life expectancy, children starting school in 2015 will expect to live to an average age of 100 or more. Knowing and expecting that length of life will temper expectations for life and for work. They will approach school with different needs and life plans. Learners will need more than ever to master higher order cognitive, affective, and social skills that have not been nearly as necessary to the industrial societies of the past but which will become more vital as the knowledge-based economy evolves. It is impossible to enumerate all the ways children will be different in 2015, but these are some of the things that the schools of the period will have to understand and accommodate.

PARENTS OF THE DIGITAL AGE

Parents of children entering K–12 schools in 2015 will also be different. They will understand as no group of parents in history has that excellence in education is the key to happiness and success in life. They will understand because they will have witnessed it firsthand in their own lives and careers. They will not hesitate to blend and mix educational opportunities afforded by schools; commercial and public distributed learning services; private tutors, counselors, and diagnosticians; and travel experiences offered by an environmental and educational tourism industry in full flower at the time.

GOOD-BYE TO STANDARDS-BASED LEARNING

By 2015, the education-consuming public will have driven the last nail in the movement to make standards of learning the driving force in K–12 educational practice. In 2001, the standards movement represents the last gasp of our old analog society to make the future fit its mold and its vision. Emphasis on test scores and improvement in learning particular bits of content will have disappeared by 2015. In contrast to the cultural literacy movement of the 1990s, a new movement will focus on developing particular skill sets and behavioral and attitudinal qualities that foster career success through lifelong learning and the ability to accommodate change. Parents, in general, will accept the belief that the mission of schools is to impart not a shared knowledge or cultural background but, rather, a shared ethic and vision for humankind's future that sustains a global society and prepares for an interplanetary and interstellar one that will suddenly seem close enough to actually reach.

Parents will be more involved in the learning lives of their children. Those institutions that offer services to all age groups will be the most successful. Parents will frequently attend "school" with their children as institutions leverage very heavy investments in new resources by reaching out to all age groups. The fusion of institutions that began in the 2008–14 period will have fully assimilated the home by 2015. Whereas the locus of control of learning content was the school in the period 2001–07, by 2021, it will be the home that controls content, as parents in partnership with their children make informed choices about what learning services and resources to use for any given element of a learning plan.

GLOBAL SOCIETY

The communications revolution that has accompanied the computer and its interconnected maze of networks has brought the world to our desktops and our desktops to the world. Not only will U.S. students have access to e-learning technologies, so will students in all nations. Competition for everything including jobs, the best places to live, goods, and services will increase. Competition will push the value of learning forward in the minds of students as never before. Having an advantage in life will be less and less left to the circumstances of birth and more and more the result of ambition and learning with access to the most powerful information tools and resources.

LEARNING TECHNOLOGY IN 2015

If we have to pick one new buzz word that will present itself as the educational panacea of the day it would be *simulation* or whatever term is used at the time to describe the process. One has only to look at the capabilities of the inexpensive Sony Playstation II, introduced in 2000, to begin to appreciate the capabilities of systems with another fifteen years of technical evolution behind them. The increasing power of computers will make realistic and highly interactive simulations more effective and more available to support learning. Traditional schools and classrooms may not be best suited for the operation and maintenance of these, however. Expect museums and commercial sites to offer the high-end range of these services instead. Schools may offer some, but the best will be supported by consumerism.

VIRTUAL REALITY ARRIVES

Virtual reality (VR) will have assumed a major role in learning software by 2014. Just as special theaters provide the iMax movie experience today, special theaters or museums will provide VR simulations by 2015. We may even end up calling them "holodecks," keeping alive the vision Gene Roddenberry made a part of the *Star Trek* television series and movies.

The VR experience will certainly have grown beyond the primitive applications common in 2001.

Traditionally, *virtual reality* has been defined as an artificial environment created with powerful computers and highly sophisticated software. By 2021, VR will incorporate sophisticated machine intelligence capable of learning from the interaction that occurs as it is used and, based on that learning, extend and refine the model it represents. Today VR tools are used to present models or constructions to users in ways that appear and even feel real. In the holodecks of 2021, participants will not have to don the cumbersome and restrictive gloves, earphones, and glasses typical of VR applications today. Special clothing, perhaps, will replace some of these, but others will be replaced by new capabilities of sensors, probes, and the software itself.

There will be definite advantages to the use of VR in learning. Many scientific phenomena are three dimensional in nature. Trying to understand these by referencing a two-dimensional figure in a textbook or on a video screen can cause misconceptions, and they in turn are not always easy to unlearn. VR technology will enable the learner to go inside phenomena and experience them from different vantage points. Virtual reality will open the possibility of new kinds of experiential learning and most likely will lead to new kinds of knowledge and awareness.

MICROWORLDS

The role that schools come to play in using VR to support learning may be to provide tools and support for learners to create what have been called microworlds similar to the way they use desktop computers to produce multimedia presentations for their classes today. In 2001, to create sophisticated VR microworlds requires the power of supercomputers that can translate models of complex processes into patterns that learners will find meaningful. By 2021, that same power will be available in basic computing devices available to schools and learners. Learning activities centered around VR may require students to construct simulations that model past civilizations or events in history and the individuals who shaped them, or they may be future or present oriented as they focus on societal problems and potentials. Microworlds will enable learners to test hypotheses, build models, and ask very complex "what if" questions. In this sense, learners at an early age may participate in societal decisions to a degree not conceived in prior times. Their participation will be logical given the investigations they can make using vast databases of environmental, social demographic, and economic data. They will have more time and more powerful tools to develop deeper understanding of contemporary events than ever before.

VISUALIZATION

The power of virtual reality to provide models will bring new scientific techniques to the hands of K–12 learners. Chief among these will be the technique of scientific visualization, or "sci-vis," as it is sometimes called. Using images rendered in animated three-dimensional graphics, natural phenomena can be examined up close. Tornadoes, avalanches, and other natural phenomena are logical candidates for visualization techniques. So are many abstract concepts in mathematics and physics. What may have been difficult to master in a text-based world may become easily knowable using visualization techniques. Scientific visualization is a contemporary phenomenon in 2001. Georgia Tech University maintains a website that monitors developments in the field. At publication, the site was located at http://www.cc.gatech.edu/scivis/scivis_home.html. Inevitably, in 2021 learners will be faced with learning more complex conceptual material. The trend that is now decades old to invest in interactive museum exhibits portends an exciting role for them to play in providing learning services in the future.

PROJECT DEVELOPMENT STATIONS

While museums and commercial theaters may offer the most sophisticated VR and microworld experiences, schools are likely to host levels of technology resources that homes cannot afford. We believe that while learners will experience the VR productions of others as part of their learning, they will spend even more time in the construction of simulations and models as part of their learning programs from grade 4 throughout their formal education years. Schools will provide access to more powerful computers and software and offer adult consultation on matters of design and construction. Mentors and counselors will monitor safety, answer questions, make suggestions as needed, and join with parents and the community to review and assess results.

The socialization and collaboration skills that will attend participation in group collaborative activities will be central to the school curriculum of the time. The development of affective skills and abilities will carry a higher value than the cognitive content that learners may assimilate during the project. Mentors may be ad hoc members of faculties on loan from government or business for particularly complex projects. Some may be contracted from learning personnel service agencies for a particular project or group of projects. Core faculties at such schools are likely to be very small and will serve to supervise and manage other temporary adults who are using the school facilities to work with small groups. The revenue that sustains the school and its core staff may come primarily from fees charged to individuals and groups carrying out approved (for course accreditation purposes) projects. Funding to pay the commercial providers will come from vouchers or other systems of funding for education at the time, such as tax credits to corporations that provide learning services at no charge.

DROP IN/DROP OUT ATTENDANCE PATTERNS BEYOND GRADE 6

Flexible schedules that extend the school day to double its current length will enable students to choose what time of the day or what days of the week they attend school for certain parts of their formal educational experience. In many cases the work schedules of parents will determine the school attendance of children. Accommodation of attendance patterns and preferences will be just another of the personalized services that learning service providers will have to provide in this prosumer-driven learning market.

PERSONAL LEARNING ASSISTANTS

Apple Computer, as early as the 1990s, introduced the concept of personal digital assistants or PDAs in a videotape produced for its Imagine Series. Others adopted the PDA label, but none will envision what these tools could do for individuals until the power of processors for the mass market reaches a level such that the software can incorporate artificial intelligence routines. This could happen around 2015. The PDA as conceived during the height of the Industrial Age was a robot that would do the manual labor of cleaning, cooking, running errands, and so on. The PDA Apple introduced in simulated form in the mid-1990s was as much software as it was hardware. It was designed to help its owner cope with overwhelming amounts of information being generated every day. The assistant found and filtered information from all over the globe and organized it into the user's preferred format. It remembered important dates, watched investments, summarized books, made reservations for the theater and dinner, paid bills when they were due, and monitored the health and happiness of its subject.

PDAs of 2021 will also assume the role of facilitating the lifelong learning of their subjects into their repertoire of services. These assistants will know all the tests the learner has taken and retain all the notes made during class, on educational excursions, or while reading. Further, the assistant will know in minute detail what the individualized learning plan for the subject is and will both monitor and help implement it throughout life. Much of the digital content will be mined from global networks and presented at the most optimum time for the subject to master it.

The technology for PDAs is developing rapidly, in terms of both hardware and software. Chip makers are learning how to mass produce customized computer chips that could lead to customized IT devices such as digital assistants. By 2021, fitting children soon after birth with digital assistants could become a major industry. Data and metadata will be collected throughout the early years of infancy and early childhood and on throughout life. The assistant will know about how the eyes move as the subject reads and will offer suggestions and exercises to improve reading rates and retention. The assistant may also "remember" a full medical history of its subject and monitor the vital life signs moment by moment. The assistant will lend new credence to the belief that there is far greater leverage in knowing how as opposed to knowing what. Its deep databanks will take care of the what as the subject extends his or her mental abilities in analysis, synthesis, and evaluation. How information retained by the assistant will be retrieved will vary. It could be displayed on monitors, heads-up displays built into glasses or contact lenses, or virtual monitors projected into the eye, or we may have techniques to interface the digital device directly with the human brain. The latter may be longer in coming, but the idea has existed for decades and will likely be realized by 2050 if not earlier.

The assistant will be one's closest adviser, confidant, and personal consultant. The assistant will serve from birth until its subject's death, whereupon it will go to continue its "life" in a vast database that can be drawn on by posterity. What you are may die, but what you knew will live on for others to use. One reason for creating assistants in the first place will be to capture and leverage the collective knowledge of our species.

8

Defining the Social
Value of School

In the final analysis, we may find it a better idea to build improved children instead of trying to invent a system of learning for the old model.

DISCIPLINE, PLACE, AND TIME

Build a better child? With the recent advances in genetic science, it may prove to be easier than building an entirely new institution to support child and adolescent development based on the old model. Certainly, education in America has shown that it can withstand strong forces pushing it toward reform. That is because the institution of K–12 education in both its public and private form in the United States serves as more than a place for learning the content of the several academic disciplines and industrial trades. Inevitably, many learning activities for the K–12 age group will shift to other, technology-driven venues as they assume progressively more of the academic functions of schools. The shift will gather momentum as the twenty-first century progresses. However, K–12 education as an institution and as a physical place in the community will likely continue beyond 2021 and, perhaps, past midcentury. There are several reasons for this, and the critics seldom take time to consider them. This is not to say that the schools, those who work in them, and the learners themselves will not be different. Here, we discuss some of the social values that communities associate with their schools and the difficulty of finding another institution to take their place.

In addition to attending to the cognitive and intellectual development of learners, the U.S. education system has served other purposes that no other institution, technologically based or otherwise, is in a position to meet. Schools teach discipline, and they provide both a time and a place when and where the primary expectation is to learn. Some homes have taken on these tasks successfully, but not every family is equipped to do so. Schools are formal, disciplined places, and most parents continue to willingly relinquish their children to them in the hopes that they will themselves become disciplined enough to do what society requires of them. Even though many content learning alternatives will be available, someone or some group has to take on the task of focusing the energies of millions of young bodies and minds on the process of learning specific and complex things. Discipline sustains the effort over time. Without schools, where will sustained discipline and sustained effort to learn come from? Which of our institutions is ready to assume that role? What new institution can we build that would do a better job?

Learning is natural, and people are always learning from whatever context in which they find themselves. Purposeful learning that is intended to master complex concepts and content, on the other hand, requires discipline, focus, and the absence of distractions. Is it reasonable to turn learners loose in an environment rich with content—real and virtual experiences—and expect them to sustain the focus they need to accomplish complex intellectual tasks, one after the other, until they reach a level of education that makes them ready to take on the world as adults? Childhood and adolescence are filled with temptations and distractions. Providing a place and a structure to maintain focus and discipline and lock out distractions is part of the unspoken agenda that continues to keep K–12 education and its schools in business. The task has never been and never will be simple or easy, as any teacher or home-schooling parent will readily tell you.

Even though IT brings access to rich, new information resources, services, and tools and to experts, the question remains: "Are business people, museum personnel, scientists, and engineers able or willing to take enough time and energy from their careers to meet this need for millions of learners and do it day after day and year after year? Home schooling one's own children is one thing, but diverting business time and resources away from the struggle to compete in the new world economy is not likely to happen, unless K–12 learning is a company's core business. On the other hand, are commercial learning service providers going to be in a position to monitor the hourly behavior of millions of children and adolescents to address their many needs and keep them on task? Clearly they cannot without hundreds of billions of dollars of investment in acquiring places and staffs to do so. Quite simply, there is no institution on the horizon positioned to take the place of school as a physical place where formal learning for millions can be carried out. Though the particular mix of services K–12 schools offer will change and though their personnel will assume new roles, the school is likely to continue as the formal learning place for the majority of Americans.

The institution of K–12 education in America has been delegated the primary responsibility to prepare children and adolescents for life. They have been entrusted with the power to do so by utilizing discipline administered in such a way as to keep learners engaged with the task. Schools have accepted the transfer of this responsibility from parents who have willingly given it. Which business enjoys the same level of trust? What kind of business have we even envisioned that could develop such a level of trust as schools in our society enjoy today?

RITUAL AND ROUTINE

Around the school day and the school year is organized much of the rhythm of our lives, as both children and adults. Vacations, the workday, and, for those with school-aged children, a significant part of social life are conducted around schedules and events determined by school. Abandoning schools and the K–12 educational system, therefore, involves more than finding more efficient and better ways for children to learn academic content. Native Americans tell the story of how the groundhog knows one big thing while the fox knows many little things. The one big thing the groundhog knows is that you can't change just one thing. Those who tell of the imminent end of our K–12 institutions could learn from the groundhog. More than the schools will change when change does occur. The more profound the change, the bigger the impact on the rhythm and schedule of our lives.

Every society develops a process by which its children formally come of age. In the United States, the high school graduation and induction into the military are the two principal rituals that affirm adulthood. To a lesser degree, college graduation represents a life transition, though not nearly to the degree that high school graduation does. By what process will our society signal the transition from adolescence to adulthood in the absence of school? Finishing the K–12 school experience successfully represents an accomplishment that says one has arrived at a place of significance in life. The formality and ritual appended to the point of arrival, graduation, attest to the significance we give it. Arriving at that day, being certified ready when the tassels turn, represents the first formal goal youths set for themselves and strive to achieve. If we eliminate K–12 school and its formalities, what will replace them? Who or what will certify, correctly or not, that one is ready for life's first major transition?

TAMING THE SAVAGE EGO

Becoming civilized means that one has learned that individual needs must often be subordinated to the well-being of the group to which one belongs. Schools are structured to teach social values. They not only teach what these values are; they also teach individuals the importance of adopting and incorporating these values and the consequences of not doing so. Social values and attitudes cannot be taught directly as we do with cognitive content. Values develop over time and are based on both cognitive learning and real world experiences. The routine and rituals of schools have evolved since their inception to enable adolescents to develop the core values of their community and our society. How will these be imparted in the absence of schools?

To learn to function as part of a community one has to be, physically, a part of that community. It cannot be done in the abstract. Virtual communities may teach ethics and values, but they will have to be built on a foundation of perceptions and beliefs that derive from experience in the physical world. The school is the physical world that society has constructed to provide a safe and appropriate place for young people to learn to become a part of the community. Schools are settings designed to ensure that their charges will learn sensitivity to and responsibility for others. What is learned in this respect is more than socialization. It involves learning to a large degree who we are. Being placed in a school with hundreds or thousands of others like us enables our identities in the world to take at least rudimentary form. In school, we develop a sense of the interdependence of people and communities. We learn it from art, literature, and history, but mostly we learn it by being a part of the school community itself. In school, we develop our first awareness of those things that make us Americans and set us apart from the rest of the world. Will this be important in the coming global society? Will we give up the notion that school is the appropriate place to transfer our culture from one generation to another? Will we give that role to the commercial media or to commercial learning ventures? It is in school that we discover why as Americans we have been more than just a salad bowl of competing dogmas as so many other multicultural and multiracial nations have become. We learn the first lessons about the meaning of government by, for, and of the people. We learn these things not so much from books and lectures, videotapes, or multimedia lessons as we learn them simply by being a part of the community that the school has become.

SCHOOLS AS SANCTUARIES

For many children and adolescents, schools provide some degree of relief for the social ills that befall them. Schools can let a child forget, if only for a few hours each day, conditions of poverty, alienation, anomie, dysfunctional families, and the absence of emotional support that often characterize their lives outside school. Good schools, and we believe that in this respect most K–12 schools in America are good schools, let children and adolescents know that they matter and that they are cared about. School, if it is nothing else, is for many children a sanctuary for the heart and a retreat from the mean life the rest of the world imposes on them.

Schools offer moral guidance without imposing religious dogma. Schools, as much as, maybe more than, any other U.S. institution help ensure societal continuity. Giving up our schools without a qualified and proven replacement that is ready to assume these nonacademic duties would be akin to committing societal suicide. Schools are the places society provides for its children to develop their sense of community, their shared values, visions, and dreams. They provide a time and a place for them to get their first glimpse of the possible futures that await them. Children will learn much from other, electronic sources, but it will be during their experience of school that most of them will construct, for the first time, a sense of belonging to something bigger than themselves or their immediate families. The process of schooling is designed to force individuals to learn to exist within and interact with a community that is a microcosm of the world outside. By 2021, schools will have become much less academic and much more affective in their formal curriculums, but they will remain structured environments where learners go to create and participate in communities, virtual and real. School will be the primary place to develop peer groups and support groups, both electronic and face-to-face. Schools will be safe places for children and adolescents to test themselves as they begin to define their place in the world they are about to inherit.

CONCLUSION

There is social value in all of society's systems, or they simply would not be supported. Parents of school-aged children continue to support the institution of K–12 education in both its public and its private forms. That is the only reason it continues relatively intact in the face of the great change in the world outside its walls. People have accepted the high personal costs associated with change in their private, economic lives. They have accepted it as necessary for America to stay on top in its economic competition with the rest of the world. We have suffered downsizing, "right sizing," automation, and outsourcing and have watched many opportunities move offshore because of cheap labor. Each has brought stress and disruption to the lives of many. We have been willing to accept all those changes and the personal dislocations they brought. Yet in 2001 we are not ready to gamble with similar changes in K–12 education. Even if our children do not learn the academic stuff as well, we trust these places to provide so much that is nonacademic, and there is no other institution to do it—not now and not on the horizon.

In one sense, the survival of K–12 education through the twentieth century is testimony to the power of our capitalist system. The consuming public has not found a viable alternative to the present system and continues to elect with its tax dollars to build and support the one it has come to trust. Whether this willingness will continue indefinitely depends on how successful schools and districts become at assimilating new technologies to enable them to provide the range of services that children and their parents are coming to need and demand, as well as how well they assume the new roles society will hand them.

Viewed in the light of market economics, to create a national system of learning services to address the full range of cognitive and affective growth and development we require of youth, the nation will have to invest heavily of its time and wealth to build anything that approaches the capacity of we have created in schools as physical places for learners. If we are wrong, and schools do not respond to change rapidly enough, we will have little choice but to make such an investment. Understand, however, that in the process we must look at the big picture that surrounds the development of youths and adolescents in our society. It will not be enough to replace the delivery of content or to improve performance on standardized test scores. We will have to find new ways to support the total development of children and adolescents. Such a task is not beyond our financial means or our collective will, as other great undertakings in war and the advancement of science have illustrated, but the task shall require more than winning World War II or carrying out the Apollo Project—much more sustained effort and much more cost. Simply stated, giving up on what we have will not be an easy thing to do.

Epilogue

For decades K–12 education has been listening as its critics have called for nothing less than a paradigm shift in our approach to preparing people to fulfill the obligations and duties of life in the coming global society. The term *paradigm shift* may be too fancy a phrase to explain what they intended. A paradigm shift is just a new game with a new set of rules. Usually, new players or outsiders are needed to come in and change the rules and make a new game. Insiders are seldom able to make it happen. How can they change the paradigm if they are captured within it and sustained by it?

We believe that K–12 education will undergo at least one paradigm shift by 2021. The forces bringing it about are coming from outside the K–12 education establishment. Society has been unreasonable in expecting the institution to change itself. American society has been pretty comfortable with the old system, and that implies that things will have to get much more uncomfortable before real change occurs. They probably will get more uncomfortable. The pressures on families and people to learn more in less time and the lifelong need to be flexible and keep on the edge of new opportunities will make things very uncomfortable. The result will leave little room or little justification for most of the services and practices of the old model, but we will retain the place, under local control, called school.

While the schoolhouses themselves will still exist and learners will still spend time there, the institution and the people who serve it will not be the same. Our predecessors have prophesized that a new system was just over the horizon only to discover, over the horizon, the old institution still muddling along. It is not that they were wrong, just that their timing was.

K–12 institutions have prevailed in the face of sweeping societal change for several decades because there was no good answer to the question, "What other group or other institution can we use to educate our youth?" The answer is: "This is all we have." They were right. There has been no reasonable alternative to the present system, but bit by bit, alternatives have been developing and will continue to develop. Fueled by new technology and new communities to serve, the old world of K–12 education will end, in the words of T. S. Eliot, "not with a bang, but with a whimper." Sometime after 2021, we will wake up and realize that we have adjusted our individual lives and expectations and in the process have created that for which we have longed.

Index